THE
MORMON
WAY OF
DOING
BUSINESS

THE
MORMON
WAY OF
DOING
BUSINESS

LEADERSHIP AND SUCCESS
THROUGH FAITH AND FAMILY

JEFF BENEDICT

NEW YORK   BOSTON

Warner Business Books
Hachette Book Group USA
1271 Avenue of the Americas
New York, NY 10020

Visit our Web site at www.HachetteBookGroupUSA.com.

Warner Business Books is an imprint of Warner Books, Inc.
Warner Business Books is a trademark of Time Warner Inc. or an affiliated company.
Used under license by Hachette Book Group USA,
which is not affiliated with Time Warner Inc.

Printed in the United States of America

First Edition: January 2007

10 9 8 7 6 5 4 3 2 1

Library of Congress Cataloging-in-Publication Data

Benedict, Jeff.
     The Mormon way of doing business : leadership and success through faith and family /
Jeff Benedict. — 1st ed.
          p. cm.
     Includes index.
     ISBN-13: 978-0-446-57859-2
     ISBN-10: 0-446-57859-2
     1. Executives—United States—Biography. 2. Businessmen—United States—Conduct of life.
3. Family—Religious aspects—Mormon Church. 4. Leadership—Religious aspects—
Mormon Church. 5. Success in business—Religious aspects—Mormon Church. I. Title.
     HD38.25.U6B457   2007
     658.4'092—dc22
2006010674

Book design by Charles Sutherland

To Mother

On my eighteenth birthday you wrote me a letter. In it you recalled my birth and "the pain and heartache accompanying it." You were only nineteen then, a mere child yourself. I was born with a failing lung and given a fifty-fifty chance of survival. "I made a promise, a deal with God," you told me in your letter. "If he would let you live, I promised that I would be the best mother I could be and raise you up to God and his purposes."

Three days later my breathing stabilized. By my first birthday you were a single mother. For the next seven years you worked long hours, found cheap rents, and got by on very little sleep. I never knew we were poor. I never knew I was missing a father, because you were such a good mother.

When I was four you made a choice that forever changed my life. A friend invited you to move with him from Connecticut to San Francisco to join a communal living arrangement at the height of the hippie movement. Naturally, I would have followed you. At the last minute you changed your mind after a co-worker introduced you to two Mormon missionaries. Six weeks later you converted to Mormonism. I followed you there instead. I often think how different my life would have been had you taken me to grow up on the streets of San Francisco. God only knows. I can just imagine.

Thank you for choosing to put me first. In many ways we grew up together. Today you are happily married with five more sons and daughters. I'm happily married with four children and doing what I love—writing books. I've always wanted to dedicate one to you, Mom. But none of my previous six seemed appropriate. This one, however, I owe to you. But for two crucial choices you made—one when I was born and one when I was four—I could never have written this one. Thank you for being true to your word.

CONTENTS

Author's Note		ix
Chapter 1	On a Mission	1
Chapter 2	Hardball Is Good	22
Chapter 3	The Road Less Traveled	38
Chapter 4	Guard Your Habits	53
Chapter 5	My Word Is My Bond	70
Chapter 6	Tithing Counts	86
Chapter 7	The Trappings of Power	98
Chapter 8	First Things First	112
Chapter 9	A Day of Rest	125
Chapter 10	What Matters Most Is What Lasts Longest	132
Chapter 11	The Secret to Success	144
Chapter 12	Suddenly Out of Nowhere	170
Chapter 13	Put Your Shoulder to the Wheel	183
Chapter 14	Simple Boys	193
Chapter 15	The Walk-away Factor	207
Acknowledgments		219
Index		221

AUTHOR'S NOTE

I am a Mormon. That's something I've never said in print. Nor has it ever been necessary or appropriate, since I have not previously written about religion. This book is not a religious one either. It is a business book about success and how to succeed well. But every CEO in the book is Mormon. The book examines how their religious beliefs and personal habits influence the way they do business. The fact that I am also a Mormon requires disclosure and has a lot to do with why I was asked to write the book.

Over Thanksgiving in 2004 I received a call from an old friend at Warner Books, executive editor and vice president Rick Wolff. He invited me to be on his Sunday radio talk show to promote my previous book. I try not to let business crowd into my Sundays, the one day I like to reserve for my family. This led to a conversation about Mormons and business practices. I shared that the dean of the Harvard Business School and several of its faculty members are Mormons. Wolff was surprised. Then I mentioned that the CEOs and senior executives at more than a dozen of America's top companies were also Mormons. Wolff knew about Bill Marriott and Mitt Romney. He asked what other major companies had Mormon CEOs or top executives.

I rattled off some: JetBlue Airways Corp., Dell Inc., Deloitte & Touche USA, American Express, Madison Square Garden Corp., Black & Decker Corp., Continental Grain Co., Times Mirror Co., and Harvard Business School.

"Are you kidding me?" asked Wolff. The notion that Mormons presided over corporations and institutions that are industry leaders in airlines, computers, accounting and auditing, financial services, credit cards, entertainment, tools, media, food and grain production, and business education had him intrigued.

He asked if all these CEOs are devout in their religion.

I told him I wasn't sure about that. A devout Mormon is someone who, among other things, pays tithing (10 percent on all earnings) to the Church; keeps the Sabbath day holy (doesn't work on Sundays); abstains from coffee, alcohol, and tobacco products; and maintains the strictest standards of marital fidelity. Also, a devout Mormon is expected to give something that many of us covet—time—by serving in an ecclesiastical position in the Church without compensation. Since the Mormon Church has no paid clergy, all Church positions—bishops, Sunday school teachers, elders, and priests—are filled by Church members who respond to calls to serve by committing between five and twenty-five hours per week to the Church on top of their professional and family obligations.

With a few exceptions, most of these executives were strangers to me. Besides their corporate titles, about the only other thing I knew about them was that they had served as bishops or in some other leadership capacity in the Mormon Church. A bishop presides over a congregation of up to 500 members and has responsibility for those members' temporal and spiritual welfare, as well as oversight of the Church's finances, assets, and properties within a congregation's geographical boundaries.

That was enough for Wolff. Thirty minutes after it began, our conversation ended with Wolff saying he had an idea. He asked me to e-mail him the names of each Mormon CEO and the respective company he runs.

I did. Two days later I was offered a book contract by Warner Books to write *The Mormon Way of Doing Business*.

Without negotiation, I accepted.

At a time when regulators and prosecutors are exposing widespread greed and corruption on Wall Street and high-profile CEOs are being indicted for fraud and conspiracy and fired for everything from looting their own companies to extramarital affairs with employees, my editor wanted to know what it is about these Mormon CEOs that makes them different. How do they manage their time? What and how much do they delegate? How do they negotiate? How do they treat employees, business partners, and competitors? How do they handle ethical dilemmas? What is the secret to sustaining healthy marital and family relations while maintaining their competitive edge in the relentless corporate environment that expects a 24/7 work pace? Do they truly give 10 percent of their earnings to the Church, and if so, why? What drives them? And how do they handle power, personal wealth, and control over vast corporate resources?

There are plenty of exceptional non-Mormon CEOs who have achieved great personal and professional success while holding true to their values and maintaining the highest standards of ethics and integrity. But this book is an examination of an unusually successful group of Mormon business executives who have remained true to their values.

They are: David Neeleman, founder and CEO of JetBlue Airways; Kevin Rollins, CEO of Dell; Jim Quigley, CEO of Deloitte

& Touche USA; Dave Checketts, former CEO of Madison Square Garden Corporation; Gary Crittenden, CFO at American Express; Rod Hawes, founder and former CEO of Life Re Corporation, the world's largest independent life reinsurance company; Kim Clark, dean of the Harvard Business School; and Clayton Christensen, a leading Harvard Business School professor and consultant to Intel, Eli Lilly, and Kodak.

This book is not an exposé on these men, their companies, or the Mormon Church. Rather, the book examines what makes these executives tick and reveals their habits and secrets to success. At the outset, I composed a series of uniform questions aimed at discovering each executive's background, character traits, personal habits, and business practices. Next I wrote a personal letter to each executive, detailing the scope of the project and seeking his cooperation. I mailed the letters directly to their homes rather than their offices.

Each leader responded directly or through his executive assistant. I dealt with no public relations specialists, agents, lawyers, or other go-between person. And all responded swiftly.

My letter to JetBlue CEO and founder David Neeleman went to his Connecticut home on March 7, 2005. Days later I received a phone call from his executive assistant, Carol Archer, inviting me to come to JetBlue's headquarters in Queens, New York, on April 7 at three-thirty in the afternoon for a one-hour interview with Neeleman.

When I arrived I was ushered into a small waiting room. A few minutes later a man walked past the open door, stopped, backed up, and looked in. "Are you Jeff?" he asked.

"Yes," I said.

"Hi," he said, extending his hand. "I'm David Neeleman."

We shook hands and he led me to his office. He took a call from a U.S. senator, rushed through a deli sandwich and cold cup of soup, and asked me a few things about myself. By the time I started the interview it was nearly four o'clock.

Out of respect for his schedule, I concluded the interview promptly at four-thirty with this final question: If not money, power, or fame, what drives you?

"A lot of what drives me is an inferiority complex," he said. Then he added two more motivators: "Being a good example and doing things right."

The notion of Neeleman having an inferiority complex puzzled me. At the time of this interview, JetBlue had more than $1 billion in annual revenue, enjoyed ratings as the number-one airline for service and customer satisfaction, had been profitable for an unheard-of eighteen consecutive quarters, and was growing in leaps and bounds at a time when four major airlines had either filed or were considering bankruptcy. He didn't explain his view of himself until months later in a subsequent interview.

In our first meeting he did outline why doing things right is so important to him. As a result of JetBlue emerging as the airline industry's darling, Neeleman naturally obtained great notoriety as its founder and leader. With notoriety came scrutiny and publicity. Two distinguishing personal attributes received particular attention: He is a Mormon and he has nine children.

Neeleman told me that the fact that his customers, his employees, his business partners, and his competitors know he's a Mormon motivates him to work extra hard at being fair, honest, and trustworthy, and leading by example. "I believe the Mormon Church is one of the most misunderstood organizations on the planet," Neeleman said. "Yet we are held to a higher standard. I have to be an example and live my life in the business world the way people believe I should."

All the CEOs I interviewed for this book expressed a sense of responsibility to conduct themselves in a manner that would never bring disrespect or shame to the Church they belong to. But no one was more spirited in his comments than Neeleman. "If people can see me not just as the CEO of JetBlue, but as someone who cares deeply about others and is a faithful member of the Church of Jesus Christ, I feel driven to do that," Neeleman said. "I'm very well aware that when other people in business have problems come up, their religion doesn't come up or attach to the problem. I think we should be honored to be held to a higher standard. I'm not perfect. But I try to live my life the same whether I'm at work or at home or wherever."

After the interview, Neeleman unexpectedly kept me another half hour to talk off the record. Then he took a phone call from a writer at *Forbes* magazine. By the time he hung up it was nearly five-thirty and I had missed my train to Wall Street, where I was scheduled to meet a friend who had agreed to drive me back to my car in Connecticut.

Neeleman asked where my car was parked. At a train station in Westport, I told him, roughly ninety minutes from Neeleman's office.

"I'll just drive you there," said Neeleman, who lives near Westport.

Over the next three hours I learned far more by watching Neeleman than I would ever get from talking to him. From five-thirty to six-thirty he conducted two punchy internal meetings, took phone calls, and approved a press release after deleting language that he felt gave him too much credit. He also joked with his staff and got caught taking candy from a bowl in his executive assistant's office.

He left his office at six-thirty and headed for the elevator. As it stopped on lower floors and other employees got in, he read their employee ID badges, addressed them by first name, and asked genuine questions about their workday. The employees gave him honest answers.

When we reached the basement floor, Neeleman exited into the employee parking lot with other JetBlue employees and found his SUV. He has no reserved parking space and no personal driver. I hopped in the passenger seat after he cleared it of papers, a few empty beverage containers, and numerous books on CD. As a CEO and father of nine, he has no time to read. He uses his commute time—a little over an hour each way to and from work—to listen to books on tape. The book CDs I saw were either about the Founding Fathers or inspirational and religious, and they included mostly non-Mormon authors and titles.

Just before we reached Westport he took a cell phone call from one of his daughters. It was seven-thirty and she was at home and needed to be at her dance lesson at seven forty-five. Mrs. Neeleman was at a church function, where she has a leadership responsibility. Despite having nine children, the Neelemans do not employ a nanny. When I asked Neeleman why not—he can certainly afford a team of them—he said simply: "It's good to have Dad around."

Neeleman promised his daughter he would be right there. He apologized to me, made a U-turn, and headed for home, telling me I was going to have to go with him because his children needed him. Ten minutes later we pulled into his circular driveway, stopping the SUV in front of the house. First, the curtains in the front room parted and a couple of tiny faces appeared in the window. Then the front door flew open and a pack of young children rushed out, shouting "Dad!" as they piled into Neeleman's lap before he could exit. Some of the older children climbed into the backseat, and moments later we were off again.

Over the next thirty minutes Neeleman shuttled kids to dance lessons and other community activities, and picked up some of his other children at various athletic practice fields and after-school activities. In between cell phone calls and conversation with me, he quizzed his kids about their day. By the time he got me to my car at the Westport train station it was 8:30 P.M., five and a half hours after my arrival at his office.

Ultimately, each of the executives I approached was forthcoming about lifestyle, motivations, and his approach to leadership and business. They put only one request to me: Don't write a book about us that is self-congratulatory or self-righteous. Otherwise, they put no restrictions or qualifications on what I could ask them, and none asked to review questions in advance.

Over a one-year span I conducted over thirty interviews with these corporate leaders. Almost all interviews were tape-recorded. Besides interviewing each of these executives in his corporate office and in other business settings, I interviewed and observed all but one of them in their homes. I also conducted over fifteen interviews with these executives' wives, most of which were also tape-recorded.

Additionally, I sent and received more than fifty e-mail communications from these CEOs and their wives containing answers to specific follow-up questions. I also interviewed the executive assistants for some of these CEOs.

Through this process I discovered some telling patterns and insightful similarities among the eight Mormon business leaders. I also found some stark differences.

Seven of the eight are lifelong members of the Mormon Church, all born or raised in Utah, primarily in small rural towns. Only one, Rod Hawes, who grew up in a rural Idaho community, converted to Mormonism as a young adult.

Almost all of them had ancestors who crossed the Plains as Mormon pioneers in the 1800s.

With two exceptions, the fathers of these executives had occupations that generated no notoriety and only modest income. They include a forester, a farmer, a paint store manager, a highway department road grader, a cattle herder, a schoolteacher, a civil engineer, and a mobile home salesman. Each of them said his father taught by example the value of hard work.

All eight men credited their mothers with having a profound influence on their success in business. A few of them had working mothers—three as schoolteachers and one as a store clerk. All eight said their mothers were heavily invested in them, instilling self-confidence, determination, and a core value set that has triggered a hard-charging, focused approach to business coupled with a high emphasis on personal integrity.

Six of the eight served a full-time mission for the Mormon Church at age nineteen or thereabouts.

Despite deep Utah roots, all of them chose to leave Utah to pursue their business ambitions, and none of them consider Utah home today, preferring the fast, big-city pace of New York, Chicago, and Boston. Five of the eight executives live within three miles of each other in New Canaan, Connecticut, and belong to the same congregation.

None of them work on Sundays except when unusual circumstances require their attention. Most of them try to do minimal business on Saturdays, too.

All of them hold significant church leadership responsibilities and spend on average ten to fifteen hours per week on those assignments.

None of them has been divorced.

Isolated, none of these facts explain the extraordinary business and financial success of these men. Nonetheless, when viewed in the aggregate, these links in heritage, upbringing, lifestyle, and priorities go a long way toward providing a context to the way they do business and the way they view the world and themselves. While all of these men were quick to point out their personal limitations and imperfections, all of them have nonetheless managed to excel as fathers and husbands, business executives, and church leaders. The fact that they've managed to balance these three areas has a lot to do with the observance of simple personal rules and personal habits.

"The true definition or true defining situation for a person is what they do when they are alone and don't *have* to do anything else," Dell's CEO Kevin Rollins told me. "What do they do? Do they do frivolous things? That's when you define what you are."

By visiting these executives in their homes, I saw how they spend their discretionary time and observed firsthand what Rollins meant. I came away convinced that the private character and habits of a CEO have an undeniable effect on how that person conducts his business affairs with employees, colleagues, partners, and competitors. My first visit to the home of Harvard Business School dean Kim Clark offers an illustration.

The first time I interviewed Clark he invited me to spend the night at his home outside Boston, a two-hour drive from my Connecticut home. The only time his schedule had for an interview was a one-hour early-morning slot before he went directly to the airport. I arrived the night before, just in time to retire to bed.

When I arrived he set me up in a guest room and told me that if I needed anything he would be in his study working on a book. Intrigued, I asked him what he was writing about. He explained it was not something he started for publication, but instead a book for his children and grandchildren. Since age nineteen, Clark has devoted approximately an hour per day to reading and studying the scriptures—the Bible and the Book of Mormon. Over his lifetime, he has spent thousands of hours reading those two books. Now, he devotes an hour each morning (and sometimes time in the evenings) to composing a book about what he has learned, a book that only his children may read. His purpose is neither to make money nor to preach, but only to leave behind a legacy for his posterity.

I was still thinking about that when I awoke the following morning and went down to the kitchen at the appointed time for my interview. There I found Clark wearing dress slacks and a white shirt and tie. Over them he had on a kitchen apron. He was washing dishes and preparing breakfast for me and one of his seven children, a son who was living at home.

When he finished cleaning up the kitchen, he removed his apron, served me breakfast, and sat down for the interview. I noted that the public would be surprised to see the leader of the country's top business school, a man who presides over a $1 billion endowment and sits on the boards of other top American companies, wearing a kitchen apron, doing dishes, and serving a journalist breakfast. "I grew up in a home where we were not only expected to make our bed, do the dishes, do our chores, and go to Church and say our prayers," Clark said, "but we were expected to be a leader and do it well. This has had a significant influence on how I think about the world and what I do and how I do it."

Then Clark told me a story about his childhood. He said that every day before he left for school his mother would grab him by the lapels and say: "Remember who you are." Then she would send him out the door to school.

While running the nation's top business school, Clark never forgot his mother's plea. "There's nothing we do here that's not important," he said. "We are educating people who are going to be leaders in the world."

He takes his job at HBS very seriously. But Clark doesn't take himself and the prestige that comes with his position too seriously. "I've figured out that this doesn't have much to do with me," he said. "It has to do with the position. In a position like dean of HBS, there are lots of opportunities where people will say things when they are really applying it to your position and the institution. If you are not careful you start imagining that they are talking about you personally. You can get yourself convinced that you are becoming something really quite special.

"So I work really hard at reminding myself every day who I am."

Clark spent his entire career at Harvard Business School. All seven of his children were born during the first ten years of his career. During that time period, he established a rigid pattern of coming home from the office each night at dinnertime and leaving work behind. He realized early on that if he was happy and fulfilled at home, he would be more productive and effective at work. The trick was keeping up with his peers and competitors who were logging far more hours at the office.

"In business, the number of hours a person puts in is not a good indicator of output and performance," Clark said. "What really matters is being able to create high-quality time and very high-quality production."

Achieving this balance, Clark said, required him to form personal rules at work that were "countercultural." His rules or some subtle variations are followed by all the executives in this book. They are countercultural business rules, and they form the basis for *The Mormon Way of Doing Business.*

THE
MORMON
WAY OF
DOING
BUSINESS

CHAPTER 1

ON A MISSION

"In business situations we get well prepared and we go in undaunted. I don't know if this is unique to the Mormon culture. But we are individuals who have a mission and are absolutely undaunted by it."

—Dave Checketts, former CEO of Madison Square Garden Corp.

"People do a better job if they respect the leader of the company. I learned that on my mission—the value of people and how to truly appreciate them."

—David Neeleman, founder and CEO of JetBlue Airlines

Many JetBlue passengers have had the experience of boarding a plane, finding a seat, and looking up before takeoff to discover a middle-aged man standing at the head of the cabin, wearing a flight attendant's apron and a name tag. "Hi, my name is David Neeleman. And I'm the CEO of JetBlue. I'm here to serve you today and I'm looking forward to meeting each of you before we land."

For the remainder of the flight, Neeleman goes up and down the aisle, distributing snacks, collecting garbage, and making a point to meet every passenger. He also writes down their comments on a small notepad. Although the passengers are complete strangers to Neeleman, he quickly establishes a rapport with them. When the flight lands, Neeleman thanks passengers for flying Jet-Blue and then works with the flight crew to clean the plane and prepare it for its next flight.

No other airline has a CEO who works as a flight attendant just so he can serve his customers and get to know them and their needs better. No other airline has a CEO who works shoulder to shoulder with flight crews in order to appreciate their job better. Neeleman does both no less than once a month and sometimes as often as once a week. For this, he is praised for his business acumen, his devotion to his company, and for maintaining a fingertip feel for the direct needs and desires of his customers and employees.

SERVICE MATTERS

Each time he works a roundtrip flight, Neeleman performs about ten hours of direct customer service and employee interaction. It's no surprise that the annual national Airline Quality Ratings study, which is based on Transportation Department statistics, routinely ranks JetBlue number one in customer service. "There are so many things you can do as a CEO to set an example," said Neeleman. "If the CEO is down there helping employees tag bags and clean airplanes, employees feel better about going to work. People will go the extra mile for you. They know I'm not sitting in some part of the airplane where I don't want to be talked to. Instead, I hang out with crew members."

Direct service to customers and working in the trenches alongside employees may be unusual concepts for a CEO or business manager. That's simply not the way business is done in corporate America. Neeleman didn't learn this unique approach in business school or by reading some cutting-edge textbook on how to be a successful leader. He developed these habits at a very young age, long before he had any thought of creating an airline.

At nineteen, Neeleman served a full-time mission for the Mormon Church. Upon graduating from high school, all young men in the Mormon Church are encouraged to spend two years as missionaries, which entails teaching the gospel of Jesus Christ to strangers and performing service for the poor, the elderly, and the needy. During this time missionaries must completely forgo schooling, employment, entertainment, and dating in order to fully devote all their energy and time to service. They receive no financial compensation, and they are expected to finance as much of their missionary expenses as possible. As teenagers, Mormon youth are encouraged to begin saving for their missions. The Church supplements whatever remaining costs can't be afforded by the missionary or his parents.

"On my mission I learned so many valuable lessons," Neeleman said. "The mission gave me this opportunity to serve and really appreciate people for their contribution."

While on a mission, missionaries are not permitted to return home on holidays or for vacations. Phone calls to friends back home are prohibited. Calls to family are limited to specific holidays. This same opportunity is afforded to young women in the Mormon Church. But just as the Church strongly encourages its young men to serve missions, it strongly encourages its young women to obtain college degrees.

In 2004 the Mormon Church had over 56,000 missionaries

serving full-time missions in over 120 nations and island states. Virtually all of the Mormon business executives in this book served full-time missions before starting their business careers. David Neeleman was assigned to Brazil. After spending roughly two months learning Portuguese at the Church's language training center for missionaries in Provo, Utah, Neeleman spent the remainder of his two-year commitment living among poverty-stricken people in Brazil. The conditions were starkly different from the community he grew up in outside Salt Lake City.

On a daily basis Neeleman would put on a white shirt and tie, along with a name tag, and enter the neighborhoods and homes of Brazilians. Speaking their language, Neeleman would introduce himself by saying something along the lines of: "Hello, my name is Elder Neeleman and I'm a representative for the Church of Jesus Christ of Latter-day Saints." Then he would talk to them about the gospel of Jesus Christ and answer their questions.

This experience had a profound impact on the way Neeleman runs JetBlue. "My missionary experience obliterated class distinction for me," said Neeleman. "I learned to treat everyone the same. If anything, I have a disdain for the upper class and people who think they are better than others."

Neeleman's perspective is evident in JetBlue's business approach. There is no first-class section on JetBlue planes. All seats are sold at the same price. All passengers receive the same treatment and are referred to as "customers."

Evidence of Neeleman's approach is also found in the way he runs the corporation. All employees are referred to as "crew members" and wear badges with their name and photograph. Neeleman wears a crew-member ID badge at all times, too. Neeleman has no preferred parking space at the office. Nor do any other executives.

When he flies on JetBlue planes, he sits in the jump seat with his crew. There is no corporate plane.

The most unusual aspect of Neeleman's leadership style is his compensation package, particularly in today's climate of inflated CEO salaries. Long before CEOs came under fire for excessive salaries, Peter Drucker predicted: "In the next economic downturn, there will be an outbreak of bitterness and contempt for these super corporate chieftains who pay themselves millions. In every major economic downturn in U.S. history, the villains have been the heroes during the preceding book."

Neeleman is an anomaly here. His annual salary is only $200,000 per year, plus an average of between $70,000 and $90,000 per year in bonuses. He donates his entire salary to a fund for his employees. Financially independent from the success of his previous business ventures, Neeleman is able to operate this way. "A fish stinks from the head," said Neeleman. "There are so many things a CEO can do to set an example. CEOs are just seen as money grubbers—they want to build the company on the backs of their people. The value they ascribe to themselves is so wildly greater than anyone else in the company that there's this king-type notion."

Before serving a mission, Neeleman didn't plan to create an airline. In fact, as a teenager he had no idea what he wanted to do. He struggled through school. "I was in turmoil," Neeleman said. "I spent most of my early school days with my head out the window. I didn't have any confidence in my ability to do well scholastically. I couldn't write memos. I couldn't spell very well. I never read books. I had a lot of anxiety about it because I didn't know what a guy could do who couldn't read or write or spell, and who had a hard time focusing."

Neeleman later discovered that he has attention deficit disorder (ADD). This hurt his performance in school. It did not, however, prevent him from serving a full-time mission. The Mormon Church will accept any young person into missionary service as long as he meets the age and personal worthiness requirements. "I didn't have focus," said Neeleman. "For a guy like me with a learning disability, I had never been disciplined enough to focus on things. The mission taught me discipline and gave me the opportunity to serve and really appreciate people."

The Mormon Church sends its young people on missions to convert people to Christ. But the practical result of the Church's missionary program is that many Mormon youth who serve missions become firmly grounded in their religion at a young age and develop a strong sense of focus and purpose before starting college, marriage, or their careers. "My mission really saved me," said Neeleman. "It was the first time in my life that I ever felt like I had some talent of some kind."

The Mormon mission experience also brought life to Neeleman's natural abilities and personal strengths, all of which are evident in his leadership approach at JetBlue. "Being a CEO is being a people person," said Neeleman. "If an employee knows that the CEO donates his salary to them—and that employee then sees the CEO helping him or her tag bags or clean airplanes, those employees will go the extra mile for me in return. They know there's not some limo waiting to pick me up and that I'm not sitting in some part of the airplane where I don't want to be talked to.

"You have to lead people. They have to buy into your vision and respect you in a way that they want to perform for you. People do a better job if they respect the leader of the company. I learned that on my mission—the value of people and how to truly appreciate them."

OBEDIENCE LEADS TO SUCCESS

Mormon missionaries are expected to abide by strict rules governing personal conduct. They rise early in the morning, observe a nighttime curfew, adhere to a dress and grooming code, are prohibited from watching television, and are expected to reserve time each day for personal study. Obedience and hard work, they are taught, are the keys to a missionary's success. Those keys can lead to business success, too.

Before being named CEO of Dell, Kevin Rollins developed a reputation within the company for being a logistics and operational genius. Those abilities have a lot to do with why Michael Dell initially hired Rollins. Since moving into the CEO spot, Rollins has instilled his penchant for discipline throughout the company through his management style. Many of his personal habits that impact the way he approaches management were refined while serving a mission for the Mormon Church.

"Since I was nineteen," said Rollins, "I've gotten up at five-thirty essentially every morning, unless I'm sick. Since age nineteen I've gone to bed early. So there's a discipline of how to act. A mission teaches you to get up, get going, and do things. I also learned on a mission that if you just work really hard you'll get good results. But if you're smart and work really hard, you'll get superb results."

Adjusting to the rigors and self-discipline expected of Mormon missionaries was not that difficult for Rollins. From the time Rollins was in third grade, his father would enter his room each summer morning before 6:00 A.M. and wake him and his older brother by turning on the light. Rollins' father would then say: "Here's what you have to do today."

Blurry-eyed, Rollins and his brother would sit up in their beds and listen as their father outlined a list of chores: weeding flower beds, working in the strawberry patch, or performing work in their yard, which encompassed over an acre. "There was a constant task," said Rollins. "Yard work was just a staple. He expected us to perform."

Rollins' father was a civil engineering professor at Brigham Young University, and he had his own engineering firm. He would leave for work very early each morning and put in long hours at his office. When he returned home after work each day, he would gather Kevin and his brother and inspect their work. "He'd go out and look in the yard or wherever our assignment was," said Rollins. "He expected things to look perfect."

By the time Rollins reached high school, his father's assignments at home increased in scope and would sometimes take days or weeks to complete. For instance, one summer his father instructed Kevin and his brother to build a walkway. But his was no ordinary walkway. Rollins' childhood home was situated on a lot that had a large, steep hill that ran down the property behind the house. Rollins' father, a skilled carpenter and cement mason, decided he wanted a walkway constructed from the top of the hill to the bottom. Before construction could begin, however, the hill had to be cleared of brush and rock. The entire task—from preparation to construction—fell to Rollins and his brother. "It was tough," said Rollins. "We had to cut a walkway down that hill, then through the brush and through the soil and rock. It taught me the value of doing something every day, sticking to task orientation, which I have inherent in my management style today."

On his mission, Rollins developed other daily habits, such as studying the scriptures. As a result, he still makes time to read for personal enrichment on a daily basis. On a mission he dutifully followed the Church's instructions to proselyte, a practice that typically entails knocking on doors. Although this is not the most fruitful method of convincing people to join the Mormon Church, Rollins followed this course out of his desire to be obedient. "I believe that whether or not you are actually doing things that lead to success, through obedience you will get success," said Rollins. "There's a jump that occurs just through doing it. So I'm a big proponent of discipline, activity, never say die, really hard work, and never admitting defeat. A lot of that is mission based."

The never-say-die, hard-work approach to missionary service had a carry-over effect to Rollins' business aspirations. Rollins served his mission in Alberta, Canada, in the early 1970s. While there he noticed a very successful soft-drink franchise. After his mission he decided to set up a soft-drink franchise of his own in Utah. He had no knowledge of the industry or what it would take to create a beverage company. At age twenty-one he enrolled in business courses at Brigham Young University and married his wife, Debbie. With financing from his father, Rollins opened the Pop Shoppe, a soft-drink distributorship.

Debbie quit school immediately to work full time at the business. "We started selling our beverage before we got our plant up and running," Debbie Rollins said.

Kevin purchased bottling equipment, arranged for trucking and shipping throughout the state, and built a bottling plant. Since he was a full-time student at BYU, he had the plant constructed near the campus, enabling him to race home from school at lunchtime each day to check on operations at the bottling plant. If equipment was down, Kevin would hurry to the plant and fix it in order to keep the operation moving.

"He wouldn't even change his clothes," Debbie recalled. "He would just dive into the grease and fix whatever wasn't working. He didn't even know anything about equipment. But he had this sense of what needed to be done and he did it."

Within a year, Debbie Rollins was pregnant with their first child and Kevin was pitching his product to grocery stores in an attempt to expand sales. Little by little he convinced more and more stores until his soft drink was being distributed throughout the state of Utah. To accommodate demand, he had to create a distribution plan for delivery and contract with trucking companies to move his product. "If something needed to be done, Kevin just did it," said Debbie. "If he didn't know how, he figured it out."

CONSISTENCY COUNTS

Missions can also be a powerful training ground to teach budgeting, time management, determination, and how to deal with and overcome adversity, all skills that are invaluable in corporate America. Harvard Business School dean Kim Clark served his mission in Germany in the 1960s. "The mission is so intense," said Clark. "You are on your own. And the stakes are high. You are dealing with life and death. It's serious."

As a young missionary Clark was assigned to be the mission financial secretary. The Mormon Church has over 200 missions around the world. Each of them has up to 200 missionaries. The Church assigns a mission president to preside over those missionaries and run the mission's finances and properties. A mission president and his wife are typically called out of retirement and serve three-year terms.

Kim Clark's mission president was the CEO of a bank. "I got to work with him closely," said Clark, who was assigned to work in the mission president's office after he had been in Germany for about a year. "He had a profound influence on me and my sense of what was possible in positions of responsibility and leadership if people learned to execute them very well."

At age nineteen, Clark was asked to be the financial secretary to the mission president, who had oversight of all the Mormon Church's assets and finances throughout southern Germany. At the time, Clark had completed only one year of college at Harvard before leaving school to serve his mission. He had no experience with finances. Suddenly he found himself serving as a finance secretary to a bank CEO. "By being his financial secretary, I learned a lot having to do with organization, finance, budgeting, and accounting," said Clark.

The experience taught Clark about management. "I saw in my mission what happens when a leader establishes a pattern of consistency and coherence across all aspects of an organization's work," Clark said. "My mission president didn't just care about the quality of the teaching by the missionaries. He cared about the way our finances were handled. He cared about the way we were organized. He cared about training clerks properly and about whether our records—financial and otherwise—were in order, and whether we had control over what was going on."

Clark applied these lessons in his management style at the Harvard Business School. "I try to run HBS as a living model of the very best ideas we have about how organizations should work,"

Clark said. "I've tried to instill in people this commitment to the fundamental mission and help everybody understand that no matter what their role (alumni relations, teaching executive education, running the MBA program, or providing support or doing research), everybody has an important contribution to make to the mission of the school. If the school is to reach its potential, everybody has to perform at a high level. There's nothing we do that's not important, because we are educating people who are going to be leaders in the world. My mission for the Mormon Church was a very important influence in how I think about organizations."

PERSISTENCE PAYS

Above all, missions teach persistence. Dave Checketts, the former CEO of Madison Square Garden Corporation, had a persistent nature before he served his mission. When he was sixteen, Checketts went with his family on a vacation. It began in Seattle and was supposed to end at Disneyland in Anaheim. But while driving through Oregon en route to southern California, the family car broke down on a remote stretch of highway. Passengers in another car stopped and helped push the Checketts' car down an exit ramp to a gas station. There a mechanic determined that the Checketts needed a new fuel pump. At this point it was nearly 6:00 P.M. on a Friday leading into the Fourth of July weekend. The local auto parts store had closed, along with most other businesses.

Dave's father had to return to work the following Wednesday. If forced to wait until Monday to have the car repaired, the Checketts would not have sufficient time to complete the trip to Disneyland.

"I'm not going to let this happen," Dave told his father.

His father insisted that they appeared to be out of options.

Dave disagreed. He asked permission to go to the next town in search of a fuel pump.

The nearest town was twenty miles away. Mr. Checketts asked Dave how he planned to get there.

Hitchhike, Dave told him.

Mr. Checketts did not like the idea of Dave hitchhiking alone on a highway.

Dave persisted.

Finally, Mr. Checketts consented but insisted Dave bring his twelve-year-old brother with him.

Dave had never hitchhiked in his life. The first vehicle that approached—a pickup truck—stopped and the driver asked where the boys were headed. Dave explained and the driver told the boys to hop in the back.

Less than a half hour later the driver dropped Dave and his brother off in Medford, Oregon. On foot, the boys walked to four gas stations seeking a fuel pump for a Buick LeSabre. They had no luck. Finally, at the fifth gas station, Dave encountered a mechanic who said he just happened to have one.

Giddy, Checketts bought it. Then he and his brother sprinted back to the freeway to hitchhike back.

Suddenly, a policeman from the other side of the freeway began yelling at them through a bullhorn. He ordered the boys off the freeway, saying it was illegal to hitchhike. Dave told his little brother to stay put and then ran across the freeway to the officer. Checketts explained his predicament to the officer and pleaded for permission to hitchhike back to his parents with the newly acquired fuel pump.

"Hop in," the officer said. He then drove to the other side of the highway, retrieved Dave's younger brother, flipped on his lights, and sped down the highway. As the police car approached the exit where the Checketts' car had broken down, Dave spotted his father.

He pointed his father out to the officer. The officer had already figured it out by the look of worry on Mr. Checketts' face.

The officer turned on his siren and drove toward Mr. Checketts. He rolled down his window. "Do you know these guys?" the officer joked. "I caught them shoplifting."

The following morning the new fuel pump was installed and the Checketts made it to Disneyland.

EXPECT A MIRACLE

Checketts' two-year stint as a Mormon missionary only strengthened his natural tendencies toward not taking no for an answer and for finding a way to overcome adversity. Checketts was sent to East Los Angeles in 1975, where he spent two full years teaching residents of Watts and Compton about the Church of Jesus Christ of Latter-day Saints. The neighborhoods he worked in were so tough that the missionaries were required to be in their apartment by 6:00 P.M. As a young white male wearing a white shirt and tie and pedaling a ten-speed bicycle up and down urban streets, he stood out and encountered steep opposition. He was ridiculed and sometimes even endured personal persecution.

Then one day Checketts' mission president handed him and all the other missionaries business cards bearing the name of the Church. The reverse side of the card said: EXPECT A MIRACLE, emblazoned in gold. The missionaries were instructed to carry these cards at all times.

Checketts had put off his college education and marriage to his high school girlfriend to go on a mission. But under these conditions, frustration and a sense of failure set in. Expectedly, his success rate was terrible.

"I got this card at one of the lowest points of my mission," Checketts said. "The notion of expecting a miracle is pretty powerful. It developed in me this sense of going in undaunted because somehow the Lord will open a door."

From that day forward, Checketts' approach changed. He got up every day and hit the streets of East Los Angeles expecting to succeed. "The sense of being a minority or a persecuted minority ties into this sense of going in undaunted," said Checketts.

Soon the results changed. The last year of his mission was a tremendous success. By the time he returned to Utah at age twenty-one and returned to studying business at Brigham Young University, his competitive nature was well beyond a normal range.

These traits that Checketts developed in childhood and strengthened as a Mormon missionary fit perfectly into his business career. In the summer of 1994, Viacom sold Madison Square Garden to ITT and Cablevision for $1.075 billion. At that time, Checketts was president of the New York Knicks, which was owned by the Garden. The Garden's new ownership promptly elevated Checketts to president and CEO of MSG Corp., effectively putting him in charge of the Knicks, the Rangers, the MSG network, and the myriad of live entertainment and events offered at the Garden each year. In 1994 alone, the Garden and its theater and Expo Center hosted 350 events.

MSG Corp.'s revenue in 1994 was roughly $400 million, coming from ticket sales and radio and television sponsorships. The Garden's primary competitor for concerts and live shows was

Radio City Music Hall, which routinely outbid the Garden for top shows. Checketts hated losing to Radio City. The only way to beat Radio City, he concluded, was to buy it.

That was no small hurdle. At the time, Radio City Music Hall and the land it rested on was owned by Rockefeller Center, which was under the management of Tishman-Speyer, one of the country's largest real estate firms. However, Radio City Productions, which controlled the rights to the Radio City Christmas Spectacular and to the Rockettes, was owned by a Japanese company called Mitsubishi Estates. The Christmas Spectacular was Radio City's primary revenue source, grossing $70 million each Christmas season.

Checketts wanted control of both the building and the production company. But he wasn't the only one with his eye on them. Both Disney and Universal Studios were interested in acquiring them, too. And both of those companies had far more financial clout than Checketts and MSG Corp. The presence of Disney and Universal prompted MSG Corp.'s parent company, ITT, to tell Checketts to back off from trying to acquire Radio City.

Despite both external and internal opposition, Checketts pushed ahead. After all, gaining control of Radio City Music Hall couldn't be as difficult as trying to teach Mormonism from a bicycle in Watts during the 1970s. He remembered the card that said EXPECT A MIRACLE and then formulated a plan.

In Checketts' mind, it made no sense for one company to control Radio City Music Hall and for another company to control Radio City Productions, which determines the shows that are performed in the hall. To acquire control of the building, Checketts knew he had to convince those controlling Rockefeller Center to enter into a long-term lease with Madison Square Garden for Radio City Music Hall. That ultimately would mean negotiating with Jerry Speyer, one of the founding partners at Tishman-Speyer. Checketts didn't know Speyer. He set out to change that by scheduling a series of dinner and lunch meetings with him.

Over a two-year period, he cultivated a relationship with Speyer, whose firm was attempting to negotiate a new lease for Radio City Music Hall. The problem was that MSG Corp. did not own Radio City Productions, leaving Checketts in no position to negotiate for a lease. While building a relationship with Speyer, Checketts began negotiating with Mitsubishi Estates to purchase Radio City Productions. At the time, Mitsubishi Estates was in bankruptcy. But Radio City Productions was a profitable business. Checketts offered to buy 50 percent of the company for $70 million. Mitsubishi accepted—a move that gave Checketts a leg up on Disney and Universal and put Checketts in a position to negotiate on behalf of Mitsubishi Estates for a new lease from Rockefeller Center. By this time, Checketts' relationship with Speyer had solidified.

Now a 50 percent stakeholder in Radio City Productions, Checketts woke up one Monday morning and said to his wife: "Deb, I'm going to make a deal to get Radio City this week. This is the week I'm making a deal."

"C'mon," she said.

"No. I'm serious. I may not see you this week. But I'm going to make a deal."

On each of the next four consecutive days, Checketts held a four-hour meeting with Speyer. At the conclusion of the fourth day, the two men agreed to have dinner that evening. When Checketts arrived at the Manhattan restaurant where they had previously agreed to dine, he told Speyer: "I am not leaving you tonight until we make a deal."

Speyer told Checketts he would have to come up to his price.

"If I come up to your price, are we going to make a deal?"

Speyer said he was willing to deal.

By 1:00 A.M. the restaurant was closed and no deal had been reached. Speyer said he was going home.

"I'm coming with you," Checketts told him. He followed Speyer down Park Avenue to his apartment. Inside, Speyer, who also serves as a chairman of the Museum of Modern Art, showed Checketts an impressive array of art. Then the two men sat down and continued negotiating. Ultimately, Checketts agreed to enter a thirty-five-year lease with Rockefeller Center for the use of Radio City Music Hall.

At 4:00 A.M., the two men shook hands. On behalf of MSG Corp., Checketts now had a firm grip on the property for thirty-five years and controlled half the ownership in the production company. At 6:00 A.M. Checketts made it home and went to bed.

But he wasn't done dealing. When he reported his deal to Mitsubishi Estates, its representatives felt he had paid too much for the lease. Since Checketts and MSG Corp. now had all the leverage as the leaseholders and Mitsubishi didn't like the lease arrangement, Checketts offered to buy out Mitsubishi's remaining 50 percent ownership stake in the production company for another $70 million. Eager for cash, Mitsubishi agreed.

Now Checketts and MSG Corp. were into Radio City Production for $140 million. But on the day the sale closed between MSG Corp. and Mitsubishi Estates, the production company had $70 million in cash that had just been collected from the Radio City Christmas Spectacular ticket receipts. Checketts was already halfway out of the deal on the day he closed. The next year the Christmas Spectacular brought in another $70 million.

Meanwhile, Checketts and MSG Corp. invested an additional $70 million into restoring Radio City Music Hall back to its original condition in 1932. By the time Checketts left MSG Corp. in 2001, it was the sole owner of Radio City Productions and controlled the lease on Radio City Music Hall until 2036. And annual revenues at Radio City Music Hall had quadrupled.

"A big part of my drive is this sense of needing to prove myself a little bit more," said Checketts. "My mission gave me the confidence that I could do anything I set out to . . . if I had enough faith."

THE HARDEST SALES JOB KNOWN TO MANKIND

"Missions cause you to be a better leader," said Harvard Business School Professor Clayton Christensen, who had to learn to speak Korean in order to serve his mission in Korea. "You go out there with a deep devotion and you are just convinced that your product is the best product in the world. You try to sell it and try to sell it and you get knocked down and rejected. You have to figure out how to keep your self-esteem and your motivation up in the face of all this rejection. It's the hardest sales job known to mankind."

Christensen teaches management and the development of organizational capabilities to business students at Harvard. Before arriving at HBS, Christensen was a Rhodes Scholar at Oxford University, a White House fellow, and an assistant to two U.S. transportation secretaries. Today he is a consultant to companies such as Intel, Eli Lilly, Dell, Kodak, and others. But his missionary services for the Mormon Church preceded all these professional and academic achievements. His mission also helped prepare him. As a young missionary, Christensen served as what's known as a "zone leader," meaning he had oversight and responsibility to motivate his fellow missionaries. This leadership assignment can be an even harder task than taking religion to the doors of strangers. "It's an even harder sales management job," said Christensen, who saw the experience as great preparation for the world of big business. "If you are a zone leader, how do you keep these guys motivated when rejection is what their life is all about? Then you come into the business world and it's duck soup compared to that."

American Express' chief financial officer, Gary Crittenden, served his Mormon mission in Germany. "The thing a mission does is teach you persistency," said Crittenden. "Every day you have to get up and say 'I'm going to spend this whole day out walking the streets,' in some cases going door-to-door, and in some cases just stopping people on the street or on busses, even in the coldest weather.'"

The coupling of this persistence with other management skills can produce a powerful, unstoppable force in business. "As a nineteen-year-old missionary for the Church, you learn to advance your views in the face of significant opposition," said Dave Checketts. "If you don't, you never succeed as a missionary. That's what makes the training so valuable and so unique."

And when these men emerge from their mission experience, they have intensity and a sharp focus that cannot be taught in any business school. "We get married younger," said David Neeleman. "We have kids younger. We don't go through that phase of adolescence where men hang out with guys in bars. We come home from our missions, get married, start raising children, and get to work.

I was married seven weeks after my mission and we had a child ten months later. I didn't have time to play around. I just had to get to work. So there is seriousness and focus."

The missionary training quickly surfaces in their approach to business. "In business situations we get well prepared and we go in undaunted," said Checketts. "I don't know if this is unique to the Mormon culture. But we are individuals who have a mission and are absolutely undaunted by it."

CHAPTER 2

HARDBALL IS GOOD

"Whether it is television, sports, or business, it's always about winning. I have always run very, very deep that way. When it comes to being competitive, I'm off the map, way over the top."

—Dave Checketts

"Down deep in my gut I hate it when someone else does something better than me."

—David Neeleman

"I hate to lose! I don't want to hurt people to win. But I want to win."

—Kevin Rollins

Money, power, and fame. They are three primary motivators behind many successful people. Success in the business world is particularly measured by wealth and titles. All of the CEOs in this book have both. They also have obtained a degree of fame, at least within their respective industries.

Yet all of them shun fame and take a cautionary approach to power and money.

"My lifestyle doesn't demand the money I have today, or even the money I had when I started JetBlue," said David Neeleman. "Money can have a corrupting influence."

Power can, too.

So if money, power, and fame aren't these business leaders' root drivers, what is? "What drives me is my tremendous competitive streak," said Neeleman. "I don't want to lose. That's what keeps me going. Down deep in my gut I hate it when someone does something better than me."

Before computers and the Internet, management guru Peter Drucker predicted the arrival of what he referred to as "knowledge workers" who would be motivated by personal pride as much as by fear and a paycheck. These Mormon executives may not be exactly what Drucker had in mind. But in one way or another, each of the CEOs said he is driven by a need to achieve excellence in his respective industry. "I have this great desire to do things no one has done before, to excel and do extraordinary things," said Rollins. "What I love to do is solve a problem, work it through, and create some excellence for our company and our customers. So for me it's the excitement of creating something bigger and better than everyone else, to become the company that people benchmark against."

The quest for excellence is borne out in a relentless, competitive approach to business. "I admire excellence, and demand it of myself and people around me," said Dave Checketts. "The competition to be the best is what really drives me. When it comes to my competitive nature, I am off the map—way, way over the top."

Before founding JetBlue Airways, David Neeleman got a first-hand look at just how competitive Checketts can be when the two of them met for the first time. Both men were running businesses in Utah. Neeleman was the president of Utah-based airline Morris Air, and Checketts was the president of the Utah Jazz. Morris Air was one of many clients that purchased advertising space at Jazz games. Checketts treated these advertising clients to a weeklong cruise in appreciation for their business. Neeleman attended the cruise as a corporate representative for Morris Air.

The cruise ship had a basketball court on the top deck and Checketts organized games for the clients each day. Neeleman ended up on a team playing against Checketts, who stands six-foot-five, weighs 235 pounds, and formerly played college basketball at Brigham Young University. Wind conditions on the top deck made it near impossible to shoot jump shots. Instead, players were frequently forced to drive to the basket and attempt layups. The first time Neeleman drove to the basket, Checketts flattened him. When the ball got loose, Checketts screamed at his teammates: "Get it! Get it!"

Checketts' intensity surprised Neeleman. Checketts, after all, was the host and Neeleman was his guest. "You'd think you'd let your customers win a little bit," Neeleman recalled thinking at the time. "But he didn't want to let anybody win. For him it was just all winning. I thought: Wow, this guy is competitive."

As a businessman, Neeleman is just as competitive. "It is every man for himself in the business world," Neeleman said. "It's all about doing better than everyone else. I have a tremendous competitive streak. I don't want to lose. I hate to lose."

Neeleman has an extra incentive to perform, a personality trait that even his Mormon business colleagues don't seem to share: low self-esteem. "A lot of what drives me is an inferiority complex," Neeleman said. He attributes this to his ADD. Neeleman never feels satisfied that he's achieving enough or working hard enough. Yet Neeleman has established himself as a modern-day mover and shaker in the aviation industry. Since the airline industry deregulated in 1978, only a handful of startup airlines have succeeded. Neeleman founded two of them: Morris Air and JetBlue. He has also been the mind behind numerous ideas that have revolutionized the industry, such as the electronic purchase versus a paper ticket.

Between Morris Air and JetBlue, Neeleman founded and became CEO of Open Skies, a touch-screen airline reservation and check-in systems company. He was looking for a way to enable passengers to purchase air travel and obtain boarding passes faster and more efficiently, while also generating a cost-cutting measure on the part of the airlines. Neeleman sold Open Skies to Hewlett-Packard in 1999 for $22 million.

In its first five years, JetBlue consistently hammered its competitors by developing a business model that exploited the steady erosion of customer satisfaction in the airline industry and found ways to eliminate cost. Neeleman came up with the idea to have all reservation agents work from home, significantly reducing Jet-Blue's overhead. All JetBlue planes are outfitted with leather seats and individual monitors offering live television. Passengers have more leg room. The airline is ticketless, the prices are standardized, and the cost to fly undercuts the competitors in virtually every market that JetBlue flies.

"I love creating a better mousetrap, creating something that people have a very difficult time matching or competing with," said Neeleman. "I'm always trying to figure out what we can do better than everyone else and how we can make sure that what we're doing can't be duplicated."

Competitiveness and beating opponents are not terms typically associated with the basic religious tenets of Christianity. Mormons are Christians who ascribe to the New Testament teachings such as "Turn the other cheek," "Meekness is a virtue," and "Love your enemy." All of the corporate leaders in this book believe in those teachings and strive to adhere to them in their personal lives. They also are extremely hard charging in the business world. Not all Mormons understand the difference.

"There is this notion among some Mormons that if you are aggressive in your position that is somehow offensive," said Dave Checketts. "In the world of business, you have to defend your point of view."

Checketts' two senior business partners are Protestant and Catholic, respectively. At times the three men scream at each other while pacing around a conference table in their corporate office, arguing and debating a business plan. "That is very New York," Checketts said. "Some Mormons hold you to this standard of always being so pleasant and so nice that nothing important ever gets done. Our strengths come from our differences, not our similarities. I want a good debate. I really enjoy that. I relish that because it brings you to the right conclusion."

In many respects, each of these men is unique even within his own religion. "I think there are a lot of things about the Church that hold people back from becoming a CEO," said Neeleman. "There is a real focus on the family and a real focus on a certain kind of living in Utah. A lot of people who could have done great things or better things didn't do it because they just didn't feel like they wanted to leave the sameness of Utah."

These Mormon CEOs are no doubt separated from some of their business colleagues in terms of their root drivers and their views regarding money and power. But they are also unique among many Mormons in terms of the degree of their competitive approach. Kevin Rollins, a former bishop in the Mormon Church, admitted he is probably more competitive than he wants to be. "I hate to lose," Rollins said. "I don't want to hurt people to win. But I want to win."

Without this approach Rollins would not be able to compete in the computer business. "In our industry there are winners and losers," said Rollins. "Everybody doesn't win. I want to win by doing it smarter, better, faster, and more thoughtful. I just want our company to be superior."

The demand for a tough, competitive streak is particularly essential in the entertainment business. In 1991 Dave Checketts received a call from Dick Evans, a former Disney executive who had taken over as the president of Madison Square Garden Corp., the parent company for the New York Knicks. Evans wanted Checketts to revive the struggling Knicks franchise and offered him the job as president.

At the time, Checketts was working as the chief operating officer of NBA International in charge of worldwide television and licensing. Later that day, Checketts asked his wife, Debbie, whether she thought he should accept the offer.

"You do not have a New York edge," she told him.

The media also questioned whether a Utah-born Mormon had what it takes to succeed in the cutthroat, fast-paced New York market. Checketts was not surprised by the questions. Having lived and done business in Utah, he had witnessed at times an insular culture that shied away from a hard-nosed approach to business and negotiations. Checketts recognized that running the Knicks would demand running hard and aggressively all the time. "I've always been willing to do that, no matter who it is," Checketts said. "There's nothing New York about that. It's simply the kind of effort and energy that is required to create a successful result."

Checketts accepted the job as president of the New York Knicks. Within weeks he found himself embroiled in high-stakes negotiations with the team's franchise player Patrick Ewing; the league's most powerful sports agent, David Falk; and the league's most successful and coveted coach, Pat Riley. Hundreds of millions of dollars and the future of the franchise were at stake. Checketts quickly realized that money—and only money—was the driving force behind the negotiations. Nothing he had been taught at business school had prepared him for what he encountered. The negotiations were rife with plotting and greed. "There were no rules," Checketts said. "There was nothing that was out of bounds."

As soon as he took over as president, Checketts tried to convince Pat Riley to become the Knicks' new head coach. One of the lures to attract Riley to New York was the opportunity to win a championship with the Knicks' marquee player, Patrick Ewing, who was under a ten-year contract. But Ewing's contract included a provision that allowed him to leave the team if at any time during the life of the contract he was not one of the four highest-paid players in the league. As contract negotiations between Checketts and Riley's agent heated up, word that Ewing might leave the Knicks leaked out. Without Ewing, Checketts knew he would never convince Riley to join the team.

With the New York press closely tracking the Riley and Ewing situations, Checketts arranged to meet with both men and their agents in the same hotel on the same day. Checketts reserved separate suites on separate floors for Ewing, Riley, and himself. His plan was to conduct final negotiations with both individuals on the same day.

The night before these meetings were to take place, Checketts received a call at home from Ewing's agent, David Falk. He told Checketts that it looked like a fourth player was about to surpass Ewing in salary, enabling Ewing the option to leave the Knicks without violating his contract.

Checketts did not hint that prior to Falk's call he had been informed by another source that the Golden State Warriors were prepared to alter the contract of their marquee player, Chris Mullin, in order to push Mullin's salary past Ewing's salary. By their doing so, Ewing would no longer be among the four highest players in the league and therefore be free to exercise his option to go elsewhere. The Warriors, Checketts had been told, were then going to turn around and offer Ewing $50 million over five years, or $10 million a year. This would produce a huge windfall for Ewing and his agent and enable the Warriors to contend for the NBA title.

Checketts hardly slept that night. On his way to work the next day he read the morning papers. A column in one of them reported that Checketts was going to lose Ewing and in turn lose Riley, who would not join the Knicks without Ewing on the roster. The column closed by saying Checketts should have stayed in Utah.

Checketts started to doubt himself and thought that maybe the newspaper was right. When he got to the hotel, Checketts and his lawyers met first with Ewing, who told Checketts that he planned to exercise the exit clause in his contract.

"You don't have an out," Checketts insisted, pointing out that Ewing was still among the four highest-paid players in the league.

Ewing countered by saying that he believed a fourth player would earn more than him by the end of the day.

Making no headway, Checketts told Ewing and his agent not to leave the hotel. He planned to hire a coach by the end of the day who might influence Ewing to stay with the Knicks.

Checketts then went to Riley's suite, hoping to get him under contract and then send Riley to Ewing's suite in an attempt to persuade Ewing to remain a Knick. But Riley wasted no time telling Checketts that he would not sign a contract until he knew what Ewing was going to do. The message was clear: If Ewing didn't stay, Riley wasn't coming.

Checketts repeated his offer to Riley and encouraged him to sign right away, telling Riley that if he signed it would increase the chances of keeping Ewing in a Knicks uniform. But Riley refused to commit.

Trailed by a team of lawyers, Checketts left Riley's room angry. The attorneys were frustrated, too. "We are screwed," one of them said on the way up to Checketts' suite. If Checketts lost Ewing and failed to sign Riley, the attorney predicted, the Knicks' corporate parent would clean house and fire everyone associated with the failed negotiations, including the attorneys.

Once inside his suite, Checketts asked the lawyers to remain in the front area while he retired to the bedroom to be alone. There he stared out at the Manhattan skyline and the comment from the morning paper—that Checketts should have stayed in Utah—ran through his mind. Then Checketts thought of his father, who had passed away three years earlier. His father liked to quote the poem "If" by Rudyard Kipling.

Feeling as though the city of New York and its demand for winning would swallow him up, Checketts recited the Kipling poem to himself. "Sometime early in your life there's a compass that's built in and is pretty powerful," Checketts said. "You either hold to that or you struggle with who you are. My competitiveness was developed very early on. But it's a competitiveness that is played within the rules. Going outside the rules just creates anxiety; it destroys peace of mind."

Checketts suddenly burst into the main room of the suite and asked the lawyers to get the owner of the Golden State Warriors on the phone immediately. Despite the owner being a personal friend, Checketts told him that if the Warriors changed one player's contract in order to enable Ewing to leave the Knicks, he would sue them for tampering with an existing contract. "I've got seventeen lawyers who work full time for me," Checketts told him. "I will bring an action against you for tortuous interference with a contract. I will come after you so hard. I don't care that we're friends. I will do everything in my power to make you pay for your actions. And, I promise you, I will not give up."

"Are you threatening me?" the owner said.

"Absolutely," Checketts said before hanging up.

Checketts' lawyers were speechless as they trailed him back to Ewing's suite. Once inside, Checketts, in the presence of Ewing's agent, told Ewing that the Warriors would not be changing any of its players' contracts. He also told Ewing that if he even tried to sign with the Warriors, the Knicks would bring an action against Ewing and the Warriors. "I will tie this up in court and you will spend the next five years watching the proceedings," Checketts said. "Now you better think twice about this."

Checketts then made a final offer to extend Ewing's contract and his pay and promised to do everything in his power to make the team a champion. "But don't try to mess with me because I will make your life miserable," Checketts said.

Before leaving, Checketts turned to Ewing's agent. "In the presence of all these lawyers in this room, I'm telling you we will not be pushed around. You have a contract with the New York Knicks. We will honor it and expect you to do the same. If you do not, we will do everything in our power to hold you accountable."

Then Checketts issued him an ultimatum. "You have an hour to decide what you are going to do. We'll be in our room."

Checketts handed Ewing a scrap of paper with his room number on it and walked out, his lawyers trailing behind.

The lawyers could not believe what they had just witnessed. In the elevator, one of them questioned Checketts about his aggressive approach and advised him not to make threats.

"You know what?" Checketts told his lawyers. "Thank you for the advice. I do appreciate it, but at the end of the day this is my responsibility."

Moments later Checketts entered Pat Riley's suite. "Pat, at four-thirty this afternoon we're going to have a press conference," Checketts told him. "Either we are going to announce you are the new head coach of the Knicks, or we're going to announce that you passed on the job. But the negotiations are over. They are over!"

Riley didn't like Checketts' approach and told him so.

"You are not the only coach in America," Checketts told him. "You have an hour to let me know. But we're having a press conference. I've already called it."

Checketts handed Riley a paper with his room number on it and walked out.

"What is wrong with you?" one of the lawyers said to Checketts once they got back to their suite. "We thought we were getting this nice guy from Utah."

Another one of the attorneys argued that the Warriors were

free to change their own player's contract and therefore the Knicks probably did not have the basis for a legal claim against them.

Checketts didn't want to hear it. "They are doing this specifically to hurt us," he told his lawyers. "Can't you see?"

As Checketts battled his own lawyers, the phone in his suite rang. It was Martin Davis, chairman of Paramount, in Los Angeles. At that time, Paramount owned Madison Square Garden Corp., which owned the Knicks. Pat Riley maintained strong connections to Hollywood from his days as the Lakers' head coach. Checketts figured that one of Riley's friends had put in a call to Davis to intervene.

"I hear you are putting the screws to Riley," Davis said.

"Yes, we are," Checketts said.

There was a long, awkward silence.

"Where are we with Ewing?" Davis asked.

"We're in a very delicate stage. But if they try to tamper with our contract we're going to make life very difficult for them."

There was another long pause.

Then Davis told Checketts he had the support of the parent company. But before hanging up, Davis warned Checketts not to screw up. The message was clear: You better not let Riley or Ewing get away.

Thirty minutes later the phone rang again. It was Riley calling from inside the hotel. "I'll be there at four-thirty. I'm going to join the Knicks."

About an hour later Checketts got a call from Ewing. He asked Checketts to come up to his hotel suite without any lawyers. When Checketts entered the room, Ewing said he wanted a mediator to decide, and that if the mediator went the Knicks way he would honor his contract.

"That laid the foundation for the next ten years of success," said Checketts. "We went to the NBA Finals twice. My approach in that situation goes back to that compass that was created by my father in a very strong family environment."

If Checketts' personal convictions had been different, his business approach would have differed, too. "I could have made a deal with Golden State and let them do what they were going to do contractually with Mullin and Ewing," said Checketts. "In other words, I could have co-opted that in an illegal arrangement and tried to save my own skin. If I had agreed to just let this happen, the compromise was that I would have received something. The notion that was being suggested was that I would share in the financial reward for this. The whole notion was that there was going to be money involved here.

"But I came to New York to turn this organization into one of the best in sports."

The combination of winning and winning cleanly in business is no easy chore. Here are two keys these leaders rely on:

#1: Compete Within Your Power Alley.

"I like to win," said American Express chief financial officer Gary Crittenden. "But we need to win in the right way; win by playing by the rules. Win by not cutting corners. Win because you are better than the other guy and you work hard."

American Express is in one of the most competitive businesses around: credit cards. "Our job is to beat the other guy," said Crittenden. "We work every day for the demise of our competition. But we try to do in a way that is based on working harder and using our business model to overwhelm our competitors."

The American Express business model focuses on getting people to purchase with a credit card, with less emphasis on lending money. "We focus on the areas where we can really beat the competitors," said Crittenden, "and we're relentless about reducing the number of things we do that are outside our power alley."

#2: Be Relentless in Preparation.

Prior to becoming a corporate executive for Dell, Kevin Rollins worked as a management consultant for Bain & Company. In that capacity, Rollins developed a very strong background in analysis and developing research. "I put a very strong emphasis on facts, on knowing facts and on making fact-based decisions," said Rollins.

When Bain assigned him to consult for Dell in 1993, Rollins quickly discovered that Dell was not a fact-based, decision-oriented company. "It was very much a seat-of-your-pants, gut-feeling company that relied on a little bit of data," said Rollins.

As a new consultant to Dell, Rollins would meet with Michael Dell on a weekly basis. For each meeting, Rollins would prepare a detailed agenda and a data-driven presentation. Some of those presentations were visual. Others were oral. But a pattern of agendas and presentations was established.

After Michael Dell persuaded Rollins to leave Bain and join Dell as an executive, Rollins helped institute this approach throughout the company. "The company has turned into a very fact-based, data-oriented environment," he said. "We are very presentation oriented."

Throughout the computer industry, Dell is now considered the most aggressive, research-driven company. For example, when Dell first began to penetrate China, it spent two years studying, reading, and analyzing the geography and business environments of the country. Then once Dell entered the Chinese market, it continued a relentless, ongoing analysis and refinement of its strategy. "We are constantly revising, analyzing, accessing, and refining our approach," said Rollins.

This same approach is applied to Dell's dealings with other companies.

"Whenever we go into any negotiations," said Rollins, "or whenever we go into discussions with partners or suppliers, it is based on a lot of facts and data that is collected beforehand. That's the way I prepare and think of things myself."

For these Mormon business leaders there is more to their approach than preparation, skill, and smarts. Their religious experience actually gives them an unusual mental edge. It stems from membership in a Christian faith that is a tiny minority in most states outside Utah. In the mid-1800s, Mormons were driven from the eastern states through mob violence and widespread destruction to their homes and personal property. With no place to go, Mormon pioneers followed Brigham Young on the historic trek to Utah, which was then a barren, unsettled desert. Virtually every CEO in this book has Mormon pioneer heritage and an acute sense of his roots.

Mormons are no longer persecuted for their beliefs. And the Church has come a long way in establishing itself as an accepted religion in America. In fact, it is the fastest-growing Christian church in the United States, and there are now more Mormons outside Utah than in it. Nonetheless, in some parts of the country, particularly in business hubs like New York, Chicago, and Boston, the Mormon faith remains enough of an unknown that it still generates misunderstandings about its history and its teachings. "I believe the Mormon Church is one of the most misunderstood organizations on the planet," David Neeleman said. "It is maligned unjustly. I feel strongly about being a good example as a businessman and doing things right. I want people to see me not just as the CEO of JetBlue, but as someone who cares deeply about others and is a faithful member of the Church of Jesus Christ of Latter-day Saints. If I can be an example and change people's attitudes toward the Church, I feel driven to do that."

The misunderstandings about the Mormon faith can be an added incentive to work hard. "A big part of it is this sense of needing to prove ourselves a little bit more," said Dave Checketts. "It was on my mission that I learned to go into situations with an undaunted spirit; a fearless attitude. I learned to expect the best, to expect success."

CHAPTER 3

THE ROAD LESS TRAVELED

Before being named CEO of Deloitte & Touche USA in 2003, Jim Quigley served as the firm's vice chairman and the regional managing partner for the Tri-State area, overseeing 3,500 employees in New York, New Jersey, and Connecticut. Over the Thanksgiving weekend in 1999, Quigley received a call from Dan Jones, a partner at Deloitte. Jones asked to meet with Quigley at Quigley's home in New Canaan, Connecticut, and requested the presence of Quigley's wife, Bonnie. He did not disclose the nature of the meeting.

Quigley agreed, detecting a solemn tone in Jones' voice. The next evening, Jones arrived wearing a business suit. Only this was not a business meeting. Besides being partners at Deloitte, Jones and Quigley attend church together and are personal friends. Jones worked under Quigley. But at church, Jones held a leadership position over Quigley. Jones' title was *stake president*, an ecclesiastical leader who presides over a *stake* (a geographical region containing anywhere from eight to ten congregations, known within the Mormon Church as *wards*).

Because the Mormon Church has a lay clergy, the leader of each individual ward is called a *bishop*—an individual selected from a local ward to serve as a volunteer clergy leader for five years. One of the functions of a stake president is to fill vacancies when a ward's bishop has completed his five-year term.

After taking a seat in the Quigleys' living room, Jones asked Quigley to be the new bishop of the New Canaan congregation of the Mormon Church.

The burden and time commitment for a Mormon bishop can be staggering. Bishops receive no salary or financial compensation, and they carry out most of their duties on weekends and evenings. In New Canaan there are over 500 Mormons, including roughly 80 teenagers. Quigley would be responsible for their welfare, as well as the Church's finances, real properties, and other assets. On Sundays he would preside at worship services.

Quigley's professional obligations already put enormous demands on his time. Deloitte is the country's biggest professional services firm and handles the accounting and auditing for 25 percent of the Fortune 1000 companies. It also provides tax advice and financial service consulting to one-third of the companies in the Fortune 1000. Besides managing 3,500 employees in Deloitte's Tri-State operations, Quigley served as the firm's vice chairman and held a seat on the firm's executive committee.

Without deliberating, the Quigleys accepted the assignment. "I promised the Lord many years ago that I would do what he asked me to do," Jim Quigley said. "I feel very, very richly blessed. I've spent many hours on my knees over my lifetime pleading with my Father in Heaven for things I needed in my life. And he has blessed me. So I've promised to do what I'm asked to do."

Within a week of Jones' visit, Quigley was both a bishop in the

Mormon Church and vice chairman at Deloitte. He had to adjust his daily routine and his work habits to accommodate the new church assignment.

From Monday morning at five o'clock until Friday evening at ten, Quigley devoted his time and his energy to Deloitte. "I tried to give all that I could and to earn what income was allocated to me and be loyal to them and my firm," Quigley said.

Sundays were dedicated to his church duties. He began working for the Church at 5:00 A.M. and he would go until 10:00 P.M. His children were grown and moved out by this point, enabling him to spend his entire Sunday away from home on church business.

Saturday became the swing day in his schedule. Quigley tried to spend as much of it as he could with his wife. But he also completed more church assignments and, when necessary, would work from home on Deloitte matters.

"I have more to do in every day than I can possibly do," Quigley said. "I can't do it all. The only way I can manage is to pick my spots; decide what I'm going to do, what I'm not going to do, and what I'm going to have others do."

The Church provided Quigley with two assistants, called counselors, and an executive secretary to keep his church calendar. That individual coordinated with Quigley's executive secretary at Deloitte.

A bishop can spend sixty hours a week on his church work and not complete it. Quigley determined that he could devote about twenty hours per week to the church assignment, most of that on Sunday. Some of that spilled over to Saturdays. He made clear to his partners at Deloitte that he would essentially be unavailable between 10:00 P.M. on Friday and 5:00 A.M. on Monday. "In planning, my partners just know I'm unavailable during that time," said Quigley. "It frustrates them because a lot of my guys work seven days a week. But they can't reach me on a Sunday. They can send me e-mails or leave me voice mails. But they would not hear from me. And if they gave me something Friday night, they won't see it until Monday morning, in all likelihood."

The road to the top of corporate America taken by each of the Mormon executives in this book is so unusual that many business-school students and aspiring executives may not recognize it as a path to success. One of the most unorthodox aspects of this path to success is each business leader's willingness to abide by perhaps the most demanding aspect of the Mormon faith: the expectation that church members will serve in very time-demanding church assignments without compensation. Like Quigley, most of the executives in this book have been bishops in the Mormon Church. Kevin Rollins had been one for two years when Michael Dell asked him to join Dell as an executive in April 1996. At the time, Rollins lived in Boston and worked for Bain Consulting, where he was the lead consultant on the Dell account. Dell asked him to take over the company's Americas Region, which included South, Central, and North America. That region of the world accounted for 70 percent of the company's overall revenue, which, at that time, was at about $5 billion annually.

At that point in his career, Rollins had never run anything except his regional soft-drink distributorship and a congregation in the Mormon Church. "That was a big leap of faith that Dell took to say, 'Okay, come in and run this,'" Rollins said.

Rollins resigned as a consultant at Bain and started working as a senior vice president of the Americas for Dell, reporting each day to the company's corporate headquarters in Austin, Texas. But he did not ask the Mormon Church to release him from his assignment as bishop in Boston. Nor did he relocate to Texas; his wife and children preferred living in Boston. Instead, he established a grueling commute schedule that enabled him to work in Texas and live in Boston, where he remained a bishop of his congregation.

Typically, Rollins would leave home very late on Sunday nights and fly to Austin, arriving in time for work on Monday morning. He stayed in Austin Monday and Tuesday, but would fly back to Boston Tuesday afternoons in time to attend weekly Tuesday evening meetings with his congregation's teenagers and to meet with his church assistants and executive secretary.

Wednesday morning he would return to Austin very early and work straight through until Friday night, arriving back in Boston late in the evenings. On Saturday morning he would report to the church at seven-thirty for early morning planning meetings. The remainder of his Saturday he spent attending his children's sporting events and other extracurricular activities. Sundays were spent almost entirely on church assignments. "It was an amazing time in our life," said Debbie Rollins. "We were able to do everything we were supposed to do and our family was immensely blessed during those years."

In his new role at Dell, Rollins shared office space with Dell's founder and CEO, Michael Dell, and was personally responsible for the P&L for 70 percent of Dell's revenue and almost 100 percent of its profits. Fulfilling his obligations to Dell forced him to take a non-traditional approach to his bishop duties in Boston. For starters, Rollins had to conduct a large amount of church work via telephone. Most weeknights he would reserve an hour or two to sit in his Austin apartment and conduct interviews with members of his congregation in Boston over the telephone. When Dell responsibilities required him to travel to foreign countries, he would do church interviews from his hotel room at night. "Kevin would call people in our congregation from Japan or South America or wherever else he was at the time," said Debbie. "I don't think people felt like he was a bishop who wasn't there for them."

Nor did the family suffer. "When Kevin is home, he's home," said Debbie. "He's very good at leaving work at work. Of course there are extenuating circumstances or times when he has to be on the phone or send e-mails. But generally when he's home he leaves work behind."

Conventional wisdom suggests that Quigley's performance at Deloitte and Rollins' performance at Dell would decline while they served as bishops for the Mormon Church. Instead, both men reached the top of the corporate ladder *after* taking on time-consuming ecclesiastical responsibilities. While Quigley was bishop, he guided Deloitte's Tri-State office through the 9/11 crisis and was subsequently elected by the firm's board of directors to be the new CEO of Deloitte & Touche USA, a position he assumed in June 2003.

Although serving in a lay ecclesiastical position puts added strain on a person's time, it can actually strengthen an individual's ability as a corporate leader. "Being a bishop gives you a deep understanding of the human experience," said Quigley. "It gives you greater empathy for what some of your people face. And it gave me a richer understanding of the requirements and demands I put on people."

At Dell, Kevin Rollins managed the company alongside Michael Dell during a spree in which revenues exploded from $5 billion annually to over $30 billion. Dell became the fastest-growing stock in the 1990s and its growth was unparalleled in growth or market capitalization in worldwide business. In 2004

Michael Dell asked Rollins to be the new CEO, a title Michael Dell had held since the company's formation. Then in 2005 *Fortune* magazine chose Dell America's Most Admired Company.

Other highly successful Mormon CEOs have demonstrated the unlikely concept that the more they are asked to do for the Church, the more they can achieve at work. They include:

George W. Romney. From 1952 to 1963, Romney served as the stake president for the Detroit Michigan Stake. During his tenure as stake president he spent eight years as CEO of American Motors Corporation (1954–1962) and was elected governor of Michigan. He took over American Motors when the company was on the brink of collapse and led it to a remarkable turnaround by introducing a line of compact cars under the Rambler marquee.

J. Willard Marriott. He was president of the Washington, D.C., Stake while growing his company into the one of the largest, most successful hotel companies in the world.

Mark H. Willes. After serving as president of the Federal Reserve Bank in Minneapolis, Willes became an executive at Minneapolis-based General Mills, Inc. He was president and later vice chairman of the company while serving as the Minneapolis Stake President for the Mormon Church.

One reason Jim Quigley made such a commitment to his church at the outset of his corporate career was the example of another CEO, Donald L. Staheli, who served in a leadership position in the Mormon Church. In 1988, Continental Grain Company, one of the world's largest privately held food and commodities businesses, named Staheli as its CEO. At the time, Continental Grain had business operations in over sixty countries on six continents. As worldwide traders, processors, and distributors of commodities such as grains, oilseeds, proteins, rice, and LPG products, Continental used a vast network of trains, barges, and ships to connect its various operations and customers around the world. They also specialized in the processing and distribution of livestock and poultry feed products, flour milling, and the production and marketing of beef, poultry, pork, and seafood products.

Staheli was the first non-family CEO of Continental. Going back over 150 years to when the Fribourg family started Continental Grain Company in Belgium, no one other than a Fribourg family member had held the title of CEO. Even as the company relocated to the United States and grew into one of the world's largest privately held companies, every chairman and CEO had been a Fribourg. As Staheli led the tight-knit, international company, he worked with top political, business, and banking leaders throughout Europe, Eastern Europe, Russia, Africa, Asia, and South America, as well as the United States and Canada.

Staheli's commitment to his church was known to Continental's owner Michel Fribourg and to the company's board. Yet they also knew that Staheli was conscientious about managing his time to insure that his church commitments did not compromise his performance at Continental.

Staheli belonged to the Mormon congregation in New Canaan, Connecticut, where he held lay leadership positions that included stake president. With each church assignment came the challenge of keeping perspective on the need to balance time and focus among work, family, and church.

Shortly before Staheli became CEO of Continental Grain, Jim

and Bonnie Quigley moved into his Mormon congregation in New Canaan. At that time the Quigleys had three young children and Jim was just starting out in his accounting career. He had been transferred by Deloitte from Salt Lake City to its Manhattan office.

With Quigley's accounting background, the bishop of the New Canaan ward asked him to be the congregation's finance clerk. In that capacity, Quigley was assigned to account for all of his congregation's finances, including the donations collected each week from members. He was assigned to work alongside Don Staheli, then a member of the New Canaan bishopric.

During the week Quigley worked as an accountant for Deloitte. But on Sundays and Tuesday nights, he and Staheli worked on church business. Together the two men would:

1. Attend a weekly bishopric meeting (ninety minutes) to address welfare needs and administrative issues within the Church.
2. Attend weekly planning and calendaring meetings (sixty minutes).
3. Attend weekly church services and related meetings (three hours).
4. Collect, count, and deposit tithing funds.
5. Prepare budgets, file finance reports, and track statistics.

Staheli's influence on Quigley came at a time when Quigley was impressionable and had just begun to climb the corporate ladder at Deloitte. Then the Mormon Church gave Quigley a new assignment, asking him to serve as an executive secretary and in other support roles to Rod Hawes, the stake president for the Mormon Church in the Fairfield County area of Connecticut. At the time Hawes was chairman and CEO of Life Re Corp., the largest independent life reinsurance company in the world. While serving as a stake president, Hawes took his company from a $300 million private company to a publicly traded company worth about $2 billion. Once again, Quigley found himself serving in a church capacity alongside an extremely successful businessman.

"I spent a decade between age twenty-two and age thirty-two watching really good men run church organizations," said Quigley. "I watched their management style. And as their executive secretary I learned how to help them be effective. What thirty-two-year-old kid are you going to find who is spending six hours a week with the likes of Don Staheli and Rod Hawes?"

Don Staheli is no longer the CEO of Continental Grain. He resigned that position in 1997 to accept a call to serve full time as a General Authority for the Church of Jesus Christ of Latter-day Saints. Rod Hawes is no longer the CEO of Life Re, either. After he sold his company, the Mormon Church called him to serve full time in the presidency of the Manhattan New York Temple. Neither Staheli nor Hawes received any compensation for their full-time church assignments. Their influence on Quigley has continued.

After serving for a decade as an executive secretary and in other support roles in the Mormon Church, Quigley was asked at age thirty-three to become the executive secretary to Deloitte's board of directors and the assistant to the firm's CEO and managing partner. "Suddenly, instead of working with top business leaders who had moved to New York and become ecclesiastical leaders, I was working directly with leaders at Deloitte," Quigley said. "But I had this unbelievable momentum. I had watched really great leaders be very, very effective, and I knew how to help and support them.

"As a brand-new partner at Deloitte and a new secretary to the board of directors, I already knew how to lead that group of fifteen directors from the most powerful position in the room. An executive secretary has the smallest title in the room. But you're the guy with the pen. And as the guy with the pen, you are managing what's happening in the room and you're managing the action and the follow-through that occurs after the meeting."

Here's where dedicating six to ten hours per week to the Mormon Church translates into a competitive advantage in the workplace. Over a ten-year period as a young employee at Deloitte, Quigley logged over 3,000 additional hours working outside the office with highly successful CEOs like Don Staheli, Rod Hawes, and other business leaders serving in church capacities. On more than one Sunday afternoon, while sitting in a church office counting tithing receipts with Don Staheli, Quigley thought about other places he could be and other more leisurely activities he could be doing. But he never regretted his decision. "Think about the people I compete with and what they were doing on Sundays and Tuesday nights," Quigley said. "Think of the enormous advantage I had over them. I gave up sitting in front of the TV with a remote control watching football on Sunday. But look at how much I learned during that time. It provides an enormous cumulative advantage in business."

Quigley had a superior set of accounting and management skills that propelled him up the corporate ranks at Deloitte. His unique experience in the Mormon Church accelerated that rise and sharpened his leadership skills, such as running a meeting effectively, preparing agendas, delegating, learning the concept of having subordinates report back, and motivating people into action.

After completing his term as secretary to the Operating Committee on Deloitte's board of directors, as well as working as the assistant to the CEO, Quigley was elevated to vice chairman over the Tri-State area and then became the CEO. "Explain to me how someone who has a BS degree in accounting from Utah State University becomes the CEO of Deloitte & Touche," said Quigley, who holds no advanced degrees. "Try to think that through logically. You can't get there. I had this unbelievable momentum that I carried to this position. It's a product of the momentum that I created when I was thirty-two years old."

From a leadership standpoint, serving in a non-compensated ecclesiastical role in the Mormon Church has a direct payoff in the corporate world. In Quigley's case, he went from leading a congregation of 500 Mormons to leading a firm with over 34,000 employees. "In some ways you can look at your congregation as a laboratory to learn management skills and techniques," Quigley said. "Just the fundamental principles of positive reinforcement and saying 'Thank you' will build a team that will become loyal to you. I have Deloitte partners where there's nothing I can ask them to do that they won't do. The reason they are so loyal to me, in part, is due to how I treat them and in part a result of what they think I've done for the firm."

The experience of leading a congregation requires leaders to motivate people without using money or job promotion as a carrot. "It is difficult to get things done in a volunteer organization," said American Express CFO Gary Crittenden. "People have to be motivated by things that are completely different from money.

Certainly in a business setting money can be a motivator for people. But people can be motivated by recognition, by a feeling of true appreciation, by a fun work environment, and by being part of a successful team. People want to be involved in things that they think are great causes."

Long before becoming a successful corporate leader and a successful bishop, Crittenden received advice from his bishop on how to handle the competing demands of business and religion. Shortly after getting married, Gary and his wife, Cathy, moved to Boston so Gary could attend the Harvard Business School. They had a nine-month-old daughter and very little money when they arrived. Their new bishop invited them to his home for dinner. Other Mormon couples who had just arrived in Boston to attend school were also invited. After dinner the bishop offered them some advice.

He told them that over the years he had seen many young people come to Boston for advanced schooling in law, business, and medicine. Many of them had come with the attitude that they would concentrate exclusively on schooling and put everything else on hold until that schooling was complete. The bishop counseled against this approach. Church assignments and church service, the bishop insisted, should not be put on hold during business school, law school, or medical school. Do what you need to do in school and do what you are called to do in the Church and you will benefit for it.

The Crittendens took the advice to heart. By the start of Gary's second year at Harvard Business School, he was working part time as a consultant for Bain, and Cathy was pregnant with their second child. Then the bishop asked Gary to take on a very demanding church assignment that required about fifteen hours of service per week. Gary accepted the assignment and that year his grades at the business school were essentially perfect.

"We were able to juggle family, work, and church assignments," said Cathy Crittenden. "We were a team in this. And we learned by experience that when we did the things the Church asked of us we excelled in other areas."

NO TIME FOR GOLF

David Neeleman does not golf. His reason is simple: He doesn't have any discretionary time. He's a CEO with nine children. Jim Quigley and Gary Crittenden do like to golf. But they play infrequently. The reason is the same as Neeleman's.

"It wasn't that Gary didn't like to play golf," said Cathy Crittenden. "But that was a huge commitment for him to give up Saturdays to play. Gary was a very hands-on dad, very involved with his kids when he was not at work. So golf was just never an option for him."

Jim Quigley gave it up while his three children were living at home, too. "He would go on the office golf outings once or twice a year and felt horrible about his performance," said Bonnie Quigley. "But he was unwilling to give up weekends to golf. That was time he reserved for his children."

In the case of Harvard Business School dean Kim Clark, resisting the desire to play golf was particularly tough. Clark had played and excelled in the sport as a high school athlete. But as an adult he couldn't justify the hobby against his work schedule and the need for quality time with his kids. "As the children got older, Kim wanted to pursue his interest in golf again," said his wife, Sue Clark. "So he started taking his children with him. Or he would take the kids to the driving range instead of going to the golf course to play nine holes."

Golf isn't the only leisure activity these men give up. Sporting events, social outings, and weekend trips or getaways with male colleagues are also avoided. "In all the years our children lived at home I can recall only one instance where Jim went away with his friends for an excursion," said Bonnie Quigley. "I just can't remember any other time when he went on a trip without us."

Gary Crittenden had the same approach. After fulfilling his time obligations to his employer and his church, all remaining time went to his family. "I used to tell our children that if Gary ever sits down to watch the news or read the newspaper I think something is wrong because he never sits down," said Cathy Crittenden. "He's very diligent and dedicated and he's the most disciplined person I know."

The price for an intense commitment to work, family, and church is that these business leaders have virtually no time left for themselves. "Gary's life is not his own," said his wife, Cathy. Any potential personal time is fully absorbed with family obligations, work responsibilities, and church assignments. In Crittenden's case, he and his wife decided he needed at least one thing that he did for himself each day. He chose long-distance running. The question they faced was where to fit it in. "He gets up at 4:45 every morning and exercises before leaving for the city," said Cathy. "So he does it at a time when it doesn't impinge on his work or his family." This is a routine Crittenden has had for over twenty years.

The willingness to give up their already limited personal time to serve in ecclesiastical positions is demanding. But the payoff is big: increased performance at work and increased happiness at home. To these executives everything else is secondary.

CHAPTER 4

GUARD YOUR HABITS

"The true defining situation for a person is what they do when they are alone and don't have to do anything else. What do they do? Do they do frivolous things? That's when you define what you are."
— Kevin Rollins, CEO of Dell

The most famous Mormon name in business is Marriott. J. W. Marriott, a devout Mormon, started out operating a root-beer stand in Washington, D.C., in 1927. It grew into a restaurant company and ultimately became a worldwide hotel chain. By 2004, Marriott International Inc. controlled over 2,500 hotels and did over $10 billion in revenue. The company has always been run by the Marriott family and has had only two CEOs. In 1964, J.W. turned the business over to son J. W. "Bill" Marriott Jr., who was just thirty-two years old at the time. His father wrote him a letter and offered two pieces of advice: (1) "Guard your habits—bad ones will destroy you"; and (2) "Pray about every difficult problem."

The importance of personal habits is easily overlooked in business. The notion of praying about difficult problems—at least in the context of the business world—is virtually unheard of. While each of the executives in this book has his unique habits, together they share a set of common ones that spring from their religious beliefs and their upbringing. The habit of praying daily is one of them. Daily scripture study is another.

DAILY PRAYER

When Kevin Rollins was old enough to learn to talk, his mother taught him how to pray. "I learned to pray at my mother's knee and have devotedly prayed constantly and consistently my entire life," said Rollins. "She taught me to rely on it for everything I do, praying for family, friends, my business, myself, my colleagues, and for our leaders in the Church and nation."

All of the corporate executives in this book pray each morning before leaving the house for the office, and again each night before retiring to bed. "There is a wonderful blessing that comes from the private, quiet, introspective time of prayer," said Gary Crittenden. "By spending the time necessary in prayer to feel that I really know what is best from God's perspective, I usually have thought an issue through quite thoroughly. I often find that my initial thought on something ends up not being what I do. Through the work required to get the confirmation of the spirit, I find something else that had not crossed my mind before."

Naturally, this most private act is never witnessed by business colleagues or employees. Nor is the influence of this habit on these executives easily evident to those around them. But each CEO's perspective and approach in the office is shaped by the fact that before exiting his home each morning he gets on his knees. Kneeling, it turns out, is a healthy exercise for powerful corporate executives to develop humility.

"It not only helps me to mentally evaluate myself and remain humble," said Rollins. "But I believe that any success I might have achieved in my life has in great measure been attributable to a God that hears and answers prayers. I believe it to my bones."

Besides praying privately as individuals, each of these leaders also prays daily with his respective family. The Checketts family has a place in their house they refer to as the "port." It is located on the second-story landing, at the top of the stairs. The house also has a paging system. Every night around nine-thirty, Debbie Checketts gets on the paging system and says: "In the port for prayer." Everyone knows to gather at the top of the stairs to read a passage of scripture and to say a prayer together as a family before retiring to bed. "It has a deeper meaning, too," said Dave Checketts. "It means your house has to be an absolutely safe place, a safe port. When you pull in the 'harbor,' nobody is shooting at you."

In eleven years as the chief executive of the New York Knicks and Rangers, somebody was always taking critical shots at Checketts. It is the nature of the entertainment industry. The Checketts children got used to seeing their father's picture and his name on the back page of the New York tabloids, sometimes underneath critical headlines. Sometimes the criticism got personal. When radio host Don Imus found out that Mr. and Mrs. Checketts had six children, he went on the air and suggested that Mrs. Checketts tell her husband to take a shower or advise him to get a hobby. The insults to Mrs. Checketts were felt by the whole family. "I always assured my family that our home was a safe place," Dave Checketts said. "Nobody shoots at us here. I don't know how I would have survived had it been any other way."

David Neeleman and his wife, who have nine children, also gather as a family every night to read a scripture and pray before bed. When Neeleman is traveling on business, he joins in this practice via telephone. "I'm confident that God values family above any other institution," Neeleman said. "It's not easy all the time. And just because you're a Mormon doesn't mean you'll have a perfect marriage or perfect family. But the Church and the practice of prayer give us a common purpose."

DAILY SCRIPTURE STUDY

Another habit that all of the business leaders I interviewed practice on a daily basis is reading scriptures, both the Bible and the Book of Mormon. Most of them do it early in the morning, before leaving for the office. Some do it on their way to work. Gary Crittenden relies on a personal driver to take him to and from his American Express office. During the ninety-minute commute, he devotes a certain amount of time to reading his scriptures. David Neeleman drives himself to work each day. His commute is slightly over an hour each way, and during that time he listens to books on CD. "It's my time to reflect and to go without the telephone or any other interruptions," said Neeleman.

Over years, this habit has a powerful cumulative effect. Harvard Business School dean Kim Clark has devoted anywhere between thirty minutes and an hour per day reading and studying the scriptures—the Bible and the Book of Mormon—since age nineteen. Factoring in his age to this routine, he has spent between 6,570 and 13,140 hours of his adult life reading those two books. That's a lot of discretionary time spent learning things that were not a requirement of his employment or schooling. But the teachings of these books have a direct influence on the way he treats the people who work for him and the way he approaches his position and responsibilities as dean of the nation's leading business school.

For these men, the importance of daily personal study is es-

sential. "I believe strongly in the power of scripture and wholesome spiritual literature in directing and controlling personal behavior," said Kevin Rollins. "The scriptures—both the Bible and
the Book of Mormon—as well as all wholesome books written by
spiritual leaders in and out of the Mormon Church help me maintain an appropriate perspective and tend to shape my thinking on
my life, my behavior, and the lives of those around me."

Besides scriptures, all of these men devote a certain amount of
time to reading other books that are neither Mormon religious ma-
terials nor business related. Some of them actually spend more
time reading inspirational books from non-Mormon religious
writers and historical biographies. The majority of the books on
CD in Neeleman's SUV are from non-Mormon religious writers
and are books on American history.

Kevin Rollins has a practice of always reading three books simultaneously. He ensures that one of the books always involves
history or a biography on a leader in the time of crisis. One week
it may be Ron Chernow's biography on Alexander Hamilton and
C. S. Lewis' *Mere Christianity*. The next week it may be David
McCullough's *1776* and a new biography on Mormon prophet
Joseph Smith.

None of these executives have much discretionary time. They
have even less time alone. Yet these solo moments are what define
them. "The true defining situation for a person is what they do
when they are alone and don't have to do anything else," said
Rollins. "What do they do? Do they do frivolous things? That's
when you define what you are."

VACATION OFTEN AND WITH THE ENTIRE FAMILY

Other than sports, Dave Checketts doesn't have any hobbies. He spends his discretionary time with his wife and children. To ensure that their time together is quality time, Checketts purchased a second home with a barn that sits up in the mountains, above Park City, Utah. "My favorite thing to do with my free time is be with my kids in the mountains," Checketts said. "We ski. We ride horses. We ride snowmobiles. We have a place in the mountains in Utah that is a respite for us. We have no phone. My BlackBerry doesn't work there. I can't be bothered. Nobody can get an answer. It is heaven because I can just focus on them and the mountains."

All of the executives in this book share a common vacationing style. Each of them takes on average two vacations a year. Typically these vacations include the entire family. Even these executives' married children and grandchildren attend virtually every family vacation. The Quigleys have three grown children, all of whom are married with their own children. Jim and Bonnie take all of them along when they go away. Gary and Cathy Crittenden do the same. In the Rollins home, the family has a tradition of taking family vacations around the Thanksgiving holiday, Memorial Day weekend, and Labor Day. "Before we return from one vacation or family trip," said Debbie Rollins, "Kevin is already planning the details of the next one."

Habits like daily prayer, daily personal study, and regular family vacations are performed outside the workplace. But other personal habits practiced by these corporate leaders are more evident at work. These habits largely include avoiding things, such as alcohol, profanity, and infidelity. These habits also produce benefits that directly improve performance in the workplace.

ALCOHOL

Obituaries reduce a person's life to a few paragraphs, telling us the highlights of what's memorable or noteworthy about an individual. After George Romney died in 1995, the *Washington Post* published a lengthy obituary outlining his extraordinary achievements in public life as a cabinet secretary in the Nixon administration, governor of Michigan, and chairman of American Motors Corp. But the obituary also reported some unusual aspects of his personal life. The *Post* noted that Romney served as a bishop in the Mormon Church and had gone through his life without ever smoking or drinking alcohol. He also did not drink coffee.

Romney lived eighty-eight years. His achievements in business landed him on the cover of *Time* magazine in 1959. With American Motors on the brink of collapse, Romney made a controversial decision to drop the company's signature brands Nash and Hudson and replace them with Rambler, a compact car. In two years, AMC's sales quadrupled and the Rambler became the third best-selling make in the United States. This bold move earned him the legacy of ushering in the era of the compact car. He later went on to serve three terms as governor of Michigan.

During Romney's era, the dangers of cigarette smoking had not fully come to light and the practice of smoking in offices and public places was prevalent and even fashionable. Today most workplaces and public buildings prohibit smoking, and many Americans avoid cigarettes. Alcohol and coffee, on the other hand, remain very popular and are widely consumed.

Since 1833 the Church of Jesus Christ of Latter-day Saints has taught its members to avoid tobacco and alcohol. That same year the Church's founding prophet, Joseph Smith, introduced what he called a *Word of Wisdom*, a health code that advises against the consumption of addictive agents, encourages balanced eating habits, and promises health, wisdom, and knowledge to those who follow it.

The prohibition against addictive substances is consistent with another principle in the Mormon Church known as *free agency*. This principle prizes individual freedom of choice, yet teaches that individuals are accountable for their choices. The influence of addictive substances can impair a person's ability to choose and lead to unintended consequences.

All the corporate leaders in this book strictly avoid tobacco, alcohol, and coffee. At the early stages of their business careers, the practice of avoiding alcohol produced some awkward moments for some of them. Jim Quigley was just twenty-six years old when he left Salt Lake City to begin working at Deloitte's Manhattan office. Shortly after relocating to the New York area he attended his first company holiday party at the prestigious Greenwich Country Club. He soon discovered he was about the only person in the room without an alcoholic drink in his hand. As the newcomer, Quigley wanted desperately to fit in and make a good impression.

"It was a defining moment for me as a very young man in my business career," said Quigley. As the party wore on, he observed that the substance of the cocktail conversation began to deteriorate as alcohol consumption increased. A few individuals ended up revealing things they certainly would not have disclosed had they been sober. "Some people were very compromised as a product of their drinking," said Quigley. "I concluded from that experience that it is not a disadvantage not to drink. Instead, it is a big advantage."

The advantages are subtle, but real. "First you avoid ending up in situations where your judgment is compromised," said Quigley. "Second, you are less likely to say or do things that may embarrass yourself or your company. You may not be as entertaining or funny. But there's a real upside to enjoying social interaction without alcohol assistance."

By the time Quigley became Deloitte's CEO, his reputation for avoiding alcohol was widely known among his colleagues and associates. He is not alone in this habit. His number-two partner at Deloitte, who is Jewish, also abstains from alcohol. "In today's world, where diversity matters and diversity counts, people are respectful of you and avoiding alcohol is a positive, not a negative. What happens is if people know who you are and see your values and see you out of bounds, they lose respect for you and you become less effective."

Although all of these corporate leaders personally avoid alcohol, none of them try to influence their employees or their business colleagues with respect to drinking. "I would never suggest that people not drink," said David Neeleman. "That would come across as me trying to impose my will on others. People know I don't drink. But I don't want to come across as pious."

JetBlue does prohibit its employees from consuming alcohol in the workplace. But the policy was formed by senior corporate leaders without input from Neeleman and was based on the fact that executives felt that alcohol use at work was unsafe and sent a bad message for a company in the airline industry. Like other airlines, JetBlue serves alcoholic beverages to passengers. And JetBlue employees are free to consume alcohol at off-site business events.

All of these leaders are diligent about keeping their personal habits personal. But a habit like avoiding alcohol inevitably surfaces in the workplace. The question is how one handles that situation without creating an expectation of conformity among employees or colleagues. A little humor is sometimes best. American Express CFO Gary Crittenden works closely with a banker from Goldman Sachs, a banker from Smith Barney, and two attorneys. These five men were having a business lunch in Minneapolis when their waiter approached with a wine list and handed it to Crittenden. One of Crittenden's colleagues took it away and said in a serious tone to the waiter: "We don't allow him to choose."

PROFANITY

These executives treat profanity the same way they treat alcohol: They avoid it, or at least try their best to. "I'd be lying if I said I have never sworn in my life," said Neeleman. "I try not to."

Only one swear word is expressly forbidden by commandment in the Mormon faith—the taking of the Lord's name in vain. This and some four-letter words have become increasingly common in today's discourse. Those who avoid them tend to stand out. "I love being out of Salt Lake City because the people I work with in New York watch their language around me," Checketts said. "They don't tell me the same jokes they tell everybody else. And when they curse around me they apologize, which I find hysterical because my father cursed all the time. There isn't a word I haven't heard in a locker room or somewhere else. But my colleagues know I don't use these words and they are respectful."

A CEO's personal language standards can set a tone, at least among management ranks. This has advantages. For example, sexual harassment in the workplace can be a common, costly problem for corporations. Lawsuits and negative publicity that stem from sexual harassment claims present a financial burden for an increasing number of companies. Sexual harassment often begins with sexual innuendo, off-colored jokes, and offensive comments made by male employees toward female employees.

In 2006 one of Wall Street's large financial firms suffered a $1.4 billion sex-bias suit after a group of female employees claimed discrimination in the workplace. The suit alleged that corporate executives in the company attended strip clubs, spent work time with prostitutes, and subjected female employees to a range of sexually derogatory insults in the workplace. Months prior to this suit another prominent Wall Street firm let go a number of executives for subjecting female employees to sexually derogatory behavior in the workplace.

If the boss uses sexual innuendo or foul language in the workplace, an environment of tolerance for such behavior can spread more easily. Conversely, a leader who doesn't act this way can send a message through his actions.

Although the Mormon Church treats prohibitions against alcohol and profanity as religious commandments, the personal habit of abstaining from drinking and swearing is certainly not unique to Mormons. Plenty of people in other faiths or with no religious affiliation whatsoever practice these same habits. Either way, subscribers to these habits enjoy a hidden array of advantages in the corporate environment, where the slightest edge can make a difference amounting to millions of dollars.

THE FIDELITY FACTOR

Perhaps the most compelling example of a hidden business advantage through a private habit comes with compliance to what the Mormon Church considers one of the most serious commandments: Thou Shall Not Commit Adultery.

Historically, the notion of businessmen traveling and remaining faithful to their wives has been treated with a wink and nod, but the Mormon executives I interviewed don't treat infidelity lightly. "Fidelity is so fundamental in our faith that you deeply understand the stakes," said Jim Quigley. "You never step over that line. And you know why—out of loyalty to your spouse. When it comes to loyalty to your spouse, the compass is clear, the idea of true north. You just don't come off the track when it comes to marital fidelity."

Infidelity and its significance used to be completely overlooked in the business world. Not anymore. In recent years numerous well-known CEOs at Fortune 500 companies have been fired or forced to resign over alleged marital infidelity. It is not difficult to see what leads to these situations. "Sometimes executives and individuals in positions of power get tangled up in these environments," said Quigley. "It becomes part of that entitlement thinking. They rationalize and convince themselves that this is the way it is, so it is okay for them. I frankly don't think this is the way it is. I think that's the way Hollywood thinks it is."

The habit of marital fidelity may seem unrelated to a company's bottom line. But the habit of loyalty to a spouse can save a company from public-relations messes that ultimately do affect the bottom line. In 2005, for example, the wife of a Fortune 500 CEO claimed that her husband was having an affair with the company's top female executive. This allegation led to an internal investigation that uncovered a pattern of questionable dealings that ultimately reached the front page of the *Wall Street Journal.* Ultimately, the CEO was dismissed and the company underwent a period of very negative publicity and scrutiny. That same year another prominent CEO was forced to resign after an alleged extramarital relationship with a female employee.

"My bottom line," said Jim Quigley, "is that I think a monogamous relationship with the woman you've been married to for thirty-five years, while it may be out of step with society, is not out of step with what is prudent and right."

Deloitte is now the nation's largest professional services firm in the United States. Trust, in Quigley's view, is the number-one product Deloitte sells. "In professional services, the entire value of the enterprise is driven by the value of the name and the reputation of the firm," Quigley said. "If you want third-party reliance on your work product, the third party has to have trust and confidence in what you say. As soon as the confidence is lost, the brand becomes worthless."

Quigley points to accounting and consulting giant Arthur Andersen as a case in point. "To this day Arthur Andersen is not bankrupt," Quigley said. "It has money in the bank and is alive and well. Why did 85,000 people leave Arthur Andersen and why did all those client relationships depart? The brand became worthless. The clients decided you can't be associated with this brand because the firm had been criminally indicted.

"If you want people to trust you, you have to be trustworthy yourself. One way you demonstrate trustworthiness is loyalty to your spouse and maintaining absolute fidelity in that relationship. To an organization that's very existence depends on trust and confidence, demonstrating that you are trustworthy in that personal marital relationship is valuable."

Quigley is known for personally negotiating retainers with some of Deloitte's largest clients. In these settings he will personally pledge his commitment that anything the client needs in terms of resources, technology, or personnel will be delivered by Deloitte. "Now, if the night before making such a promise I was down in the bar hustling some women," said Quigley, "would this client believe me when I told him I would deliver a team and help him complete a merger? What is the likelihood he would trust me if he had seen me in the bar the night before? This whole idea of validating and demonstrating trust—especially in the professional services firm that is selling trust and confidence—is vitally important to the image, the brand, and the name. You can't overemphasize that."

SLEEPING WHEN THE WIND BLOWS

American Express CFO Gary Crittenden was updating his will with his attorney when his attorney advised him to consider whether there was any chance he might divorce his wife in the future. The answer to that question had great bearing on the way the will would be worded. Crittenden told his attorney that the prospect of divorce never enters his mind.

"Many married people go through mechanical calculations all the time about should I stay or should I go," said Crittenden. "It puts a whole series of decisions that you make in life in limbo. You don't know if you are willing to commit or want to commit. You just don't know how permanent it is."

Being true to a spouse alleviates the pain and effort that's spent dealing with the consequences. "I spend no emotional energy trying to figure out how my life would be if I didn't have my wife," said Crittenden.

Without this kind of relationship, Crittenden doesn't know how he would perform at work. "When you have a senior job in business," said Crittenden, "you don't deal with good things, generally. Almost everything you deal with is the result of something reaching a problem stage. All this bad stuff happens around you. Or a complex issue hasn't been able to be solved until it gets to you. There's just a lot of pressure at work."

The ability to handle tremendous stress at work increases when stress at home is minimal. "There's a wonderful safe harbor that comes when you walk in the door at home and you love your wife and she loves you," Crittenden said. "You know there's a place where you've got complete refuge from the storm, a place that has permanence."

This was most evident in the aftermath of 9/11. The American Express headquarters in New York had been severely damaged in the terror attack, displacing over 3,000 American Express employees and temporary knocking out the company's phone, computer, and e-mail networks. The subsequent decision by the federal government to shut down the airline industry prevented American Express from collecting payment checks from its credit card customers. This stifled the company's daily revenue stream. While trying to maintain the company's cash flow, Crittenden and other executives had to relocate the company headquarters and find office space for over 3,000 employees. This led to weeks and weeks of eighteen-hour workdays from home and satellite offices.

For Crittenden, that time in his career was like being in the midst of a brutal storm raging against him and his company. Had his relationships at home been in disarray at the same time, he would not have performed the way he did for American Express. "There's no blessing like being able to sleep when the wind blows," he said. "My relationship with my wife and children is the one thing I can absolutely rely on and the first thing I can count on when things get tough."

All of these men admit and recognize how susceptible they are to human error. "Just because we have these beliefs doesn't mean we don't have temptations," said David Neeleman. "But by being a member of the Mormon Church you understand the gravity of not being faithful to your wife."

To protect against this, all of these men have personal rules that govern their behavior at work as it applies to women.

#1: Don't Put Yourself in a Position to Be Tempted.

David Neeleman limits the instances when he is alone with a woman other than his wife. He does not go alone with a woman to business lunches or out to dinner. Nor does he travel alone with another woman. These are rules he and his wife came up with. "You can't put yourself in a position to be tempted beyond your ability to withstand," Neeleman said. "As a businessman I follow these rules ninety-nine percent of the time."

There's a direct business benefit to maintaining solid relationships at home. "I've seen people who neglect their family through infidelity," Neeleman said. "When you're not right at home you are a mess at work. If things are right at home you are more productive at work."

A simple rule like this keeps the potential for indiscretions at work to a minimum. "The wonderful thing about being a member of the Mormon Church is that if you live the religion your life is really uncomplicated," said Gary Crittenden. "You don't have to remember what you said, where you were, or who you were with. That's a wonderful feeling. Lives can become enormously complicated, strewn with multiple marriages and kids that are dysfunctional," said Crittenden. "Obedience really brings happiness. When you get up in the morning you don't have to worry about all these conflicts."

#2: Travel with Your Spouse.

In over two decades as a businessman, Kevin Rollins has never been propositioned and never found himself in an awkward position involving another woman. One reason is his habit of bringing his wife with him on business trips. Debbie Rollins accompanies Kevin on roughly 75 percent of his business trips for Dell. "I'm a better person when she's with me," Rollins said. "I pray more, read more, and think better thoughts."

One reason Rollins brings his wife is that he wants her to experience the things he sees and experiences. "I want her to know what I know traveling around the globe," he said.

Having his wife along has other benefits, too. "It gives me an excuse not to work from six until midnight every day," he said. "When you are on the road, people will schedule you from the minute you get up to the minute you go to bed. I don't want to do that. So I say, 'My wife is with me. So we'll have to end at five or six and I'm going to be with her.' Honestly, I would rather be with her than them."

When Rollins doesn't have his wife or children along on business trips, he phones home every night, no matter where in the world he is located. "Frankly, it's lonely when I get done at night," said Rollins.

CHAPTER 5

MY WORD IS MY BOND

Much of what was behind the corporate scandals from Enron to WorldCom to Tyco can be reduced to one word: dishonesty. In the last six years, the public has seen a steady stream of large corporations restating their earnings, using fraudulent accounting practices, and artificially hyping stock values, all resulting in fallen CEOs.

All of this diminishes the public's trust and ratchets up the demand and opportunity for those in business whose reputation for integrity is solid. Trust—both in the name Deloitte & Touche and in its CEO Jim Quigley—had a lot to do with why MCI turned to them after experiencing the biggest accounting fraud in U.S. history.

Jim Quigley had just taken over as CEO of Deloitte & Touche USA on June 1, 2003, when he agreed to help MCI, formally known as WorldCom, overcome the damage of an $11 billion accounting fraud. The damage was colossal. WorldCom CEO Bernie Ebbers received a twenty-five-year prison term and CFO Scott Sullivan received a five-year prison sentence. The company's stock price collapsed. Thousands of employees lost their jobs. And WorldCom plunged into bankruptcy.

The company changed its name to MCI and retained Deloitte to help it emerge from bankruptcy. In compliance with an order issued by the Securities and Exchange Commission, an outside auditor had been named to audit MCI's books as a pre-condition of emerging from bankruptcy. Deloitte's role was to prepare MCI's financial statements for the audit, a process that would require Deloitte to comb through hundreds of thousands of original WorldCom records, identify each fraudulent entry in the company's ledger, then replace the fraudulent entry with an accurate one. In all, there were over 12,000 fraudulent entries in MCI's ledger. "It was the largest project of its kind that the firm had ever done," said Quigley.

One primary reason MCI went with Deloitte was Jim Quigley's personal commitment to supply the manpower and resources needed to manage such a big task. Just months after Deloitte had been retained, Quigley received a desperate call from MCI's chief financial officer, who complained that not enough Deloitte personnel were working on the project. "Jim, it is just not happening," MCI's CFO told Quigley. "We don't have Deloitte professionals here anywhere near the scale or level you promised."

Quigley had personally given his word to MCI's leadership team that Deloitte would expand whatever manpower was required to insure that MCI complied with the SEC order and emerged from bankruptcy. Before hanging up, Quigley promised MCI's CFO that 500 Deloitte professionals would be deployed over the weekend.

The promised drew jeers.

"When I made that commitment, I was told that MCI's outside auditors were laughing that Deloitte made a commitment that it could deliver five hundred people over one weekend," said Quigley.

Within hours of hanging up with MCI's CFO, Quigley held a conference call with his Deloitte management team. Three days later, on a Saturday morning, 250 Deloitte professionals arrived at MCI's headquarters in Reston, Virginia, to receive training on how to access the MCI computer systems and databases. Sunday morning 250 more Deloitte professionals showed up for training. "We then deployed five hundred of our people to seven MCI locations the next day to help put Humpty Dumpty back together again," said Quigley.

Ultimately, over a nine-month period, Deloitte deployed over 2,000 professionals to work on this project and billed MCI $185 million. Quigley and Deloitte kept their word. "MCI would not have been able to emerge from bankruptcy had we not been successful in working with their management team and helping them to recover from the pervasive fraud that WorldCom represented," Quigley said.

Trust may be the most valuable commodity in the business world. Kevin Rollins learned this lesson as a college student at Brigham Young University. While an undergraduate student, Rollins started a soft-drink company called Pop Shoppe. It distributed beverages throughout the state of Utah. On one occasion Rollins had contracted to purchase a larger order of custom-made soft-drink bottles from a supplier. A competing supplier subsequently approached Rollins and offered to supply the bottles for a much lower price.

At that point the first supplier had already begun making the custom bottles. "But we could have canceled," said Rollins. "And there would have been nothing the first supplier could have done. They would have been stuck with the bottles."

Legally, Rollins could have backed out of the first contract. "We could have gotten a better deal and gotten more money," Rollins said. "But we had made a commitment to these folks. We would have had to leave them hanging in order to go with the other supplier. And we couldn't do that."

Rollins notified the second supplier of his decision in a conversation that he recalled went like this:

"Sorry, we've already made the order. We're committed."

"Well, you can cancel it."

"No, we can't cancel it. We already made the commitment."

Afterward, Rollins learned his decision paid off much more than the saving he would have made by breaking the first deal. "I found out later that a number of people in the larger beverage industry were watching what we did," said Rollins. "They came to us and said, 'We were watching to see if you would cancel that order.' They said they were watching because they knew we were Mormons."

Today, virtually every company that Dell does business with knows Rollins is a Mormon. He says ethical dilemmas involving honest or integrity are rare. "I don't know how much of that is due to the fact that people know I'm LDS and say, 'Don't even go after him or try to tempt him, he's just going to say no,'" said Rollins. "Or whether I'm just darn lucky."

Rollins said his hard rule against dishonesty in business has more to do with Dell than his religion, however. "Anytime a Dell-owned company is involved in a deal," said Rollins, "my approach toward anything ethically questionable is 'Absolutely not. Don't do it. Don't even look like you are going to do it.' I won't even entertain the idea. That's just the Dell ethic."

When it comes to deals, no Mormon CEO in this book has made more of them than Rod Hawes, a multimillionaire who with two partners founded the world's largest privately held life reinsurance company, Life Re. Hawes was the CEO of Life Re until he sold it to Swiss Re, the world's largest publicly held reinsurance company, for about $2 billion in 1998. "I did not deal with the public," Hawes said. "That's why people don't know anything about me. It was a great place to be. We did reinsurance with major life insurance companies and small ones. We were the insurance companies' insurance company."

Hawes is from Marsing, Idaho, a ranching and farming community located thirty-five miles outside Boise. It had about 400 residents while Hawes was growing up. His ancestors migrated to the area in the 1800s. They were pioneers. But they were not Mormons. Hawes was raised Presbyterian. His mother taught school; his father worked in a lumber yard, drove a road grader for the highway district, and was the editor for a small-town weekly newspaper. At age twelve, Hawes accompanied his parents on a trip to Palo Alto. His mother wanted Rod to see the Stanford University campus. A year later, Hawes entered high school. In 1955 he was one of only thirty-six students in his graduating class. Later that fall he entered Stanford; he didn't apply anywhere else.

When Hawes left home his mother sent him off with a promise and a plea.

The promise: You can do whatever you want in life.

The plea: Remember who you are.

These were the same two things she had said to him virtually every day before he left home for school as a child. Within these two simple messages are two truths that guided Hawes' approach to business: With smarts and integrity you can go a long, long way.

After graduating from Stanford, Hawes sold life insurance for Mutual of New York. His manager and associate manager were both Mormons. They showed Hawes the ins and outs of the insurance industry and put a high premium on integrity. Within five years Hawes had become one of the top-rated insurance salesmen in the country.

In 1966 Hawes joined the Mormon Church and applied to the Harvard Business School. A year later he got accepted and went on to become a Baker Scholar and earn his MBA. After business school, he landed in Stamford, Connecticut, working for a Wall Street analyst specializing in life insurance companies. Hawes had discovered that there were about 2,000 life insurance companies in the United States. Some were big like Northwestern Mutual, Metropolitan, New York Life, and Prudential. But hundreds of them were small and regional. Seeing an opportunity to consolidate the industry and make it more efficient, Hawes assumed the role of an investment banker and began acquiring and merging life insurance companies. Mergers and acquisitions became his specialty.

"Every merger involves facts and people," said Hawes. "I learned that the personalities have more to do with it. The numbers have to work, of course. But unless you connect the personalities and they come together, you are not going to get anywhere."

By building relationships of trust with CEOs and executives throughout the industry, Hawes carried out hundreds of millions of dollars in mergers and acquisitions on the basis of a handshake. "I had no written agreements with these people," said Hawes. "Integrity is a key part of the deal. I'm not tolerant when it comes to people who lie, people who cheat, and people who don't tell the truth. That's a no-no. If you have a problem, you can tell me anything. I can deal with any problem. But don't lie to me."

In the 1970s Hawes asked a Jewish friend with life insurance expertise to be his business partner. They never signed a contract, choosing instead to memorialize their agreement with a handshake. Together they completed over a hundred mergers and acquisitions. The last one was valued at $23 billion. Then in 1988 Hawes and his partners put together $300 million in financing and bought Re Insurance Company of General Reassurance. They changed the company's name to Life Re and Hawes became chairman and CEO.

As CEO, Hawes believed that his company would perform better if his employees were treated fairly and compensated appropriately. In 1992 when Hawes took his private company public, he insisted that every employee be given stock in the company. "Everyone right down to the clerk in the mailroom got stock," said Hawes. "I don't understand people who are so selfish and greedy that they feel entitled to squeeze other people. I just don't get it. First of all, it's stupid from a business standpoint because you can get much more out of employees when you are good to them."

Hawes' approach worked. After going public in '92, his company enjoyed annual revenue increases of 20 percent. Within five years Life Re had several hundred million dollars in premiums and several billion dollars in assets. In 1998, Swiss Re, the world's largest reinsurance company, bought Life Re for about $2 billion. When Hawes sold his company, every one of his employees got rewarded. "We had some millionaires and a bunch of people in the hundreds-of-thousands-of-dollars range," Hawes said. "They worked very hard for us and were rewarded as a result."

Today Rod Hawes has a building named after him at Harvard

Business School; several scholarships in his name at leading institutions, including Brigham Young University; and various facilities named after him in his hometown of New Canaan, Connecticut. All of them pay tribute to his phenomenal business success. But adherence to some simple rules learned in childhood guided his approach to money. In his commencement address to Brigham Young University business school graduates titled "Remember Who You Are," Hawes attributed much of his success to his parents and their teachings.

He approached every deal with an eye toward the next one. In other words, he never took a short-term approach to his business dealings. Whether dealing with mergers and acquisitions, with investors, or with employees, Hawes always looked long-term.

If you treat people fairly and honestly the first time, they will trust you and want to do business with you the next time. Rod Hawes used this approach to help revolutionize and consolidate the life reinsurance industry. David Neeleman took this same entrepreneurial approach to the airline industry. Long before founding JetBlue, Neeleman helped create Morris Air, a privately owned, regional airline based out of Salt Lake City. Neeleman was twenty-three at the time and had just dropped out of college. He ran Morris Air successfully for ten years. While Neeleman was president of the company, the airline decided to go public and engaged the services of Weston Presidio Capital, a venture capital firm. Weston Presidio projected that Morris Air was worth $200 million. But before Morris Air went public, its owner decided to sell the airline to Southwest Airlines for $130 million. The owner entrusted Neeleman with the sale of the airline to Southwest.

By that point, Weston Presidio had invested $15 million in

Morris Air. Neeleman and Morris Air were prepared to return $30 million to Weston Presidio upon sale to Southwest, essentially enabling Weston Presidio to double its money.

When Neeleman proposed this plan to Weston Presidio, however, the venture capital firm took the position that bringing the airline public would generate more money than selling to Southwest. Weston Presidio was prepared to hold Morris Air to its initial promise to take the company public.

Neeleman asked Weston Presidio what they wanted. The answer was simple: Rather than doubling its return on the initial investment of $15 million, Presidio wanted $45 million, two and a half times what it had invested.

Neeleman asked if they would feel as though they had been treated fairly if Morris Air agreed to these terms.

The firm indicated it would.

"There is plenty of money for everybody here," Neeleman recalled telling them.

This approach averted potentially costly litigation. More important, it established a relationship of trust that paid big dividends for Neeleman down the road. When Neeleman decided to form JetBlue, he turned to Weston Presidio and asked if they would invest. "They said, 'With you, anytime, anyplace, anywhere,'" Neeleman recalled.

As a result, much of the initial $130 million invested in the start-up of JetBlue came from investors in Morris Air.

This approach of looking long-term and dealing fairly with employees and investors also applies to vendors and suppliers. The relationship a company has with its vendors and suppliers can have a dramatic impact on that company's bottom line. "Most companies call their suppliers vendors," said Neeleman. "We call them business partners. We pay them on time. And we negotiate with them fairly."

One school of thought divorces "fairness" from "negotiations" when it comes to business, leading to an "every man for himself" approach. Neeleman sees this all the time. But he has never embraced it. After he created JetBlue and it began to expand rapidly, Neeleman needed more airplanes. He had initial discussions with Boeing and Airbus. Then JetBlue negotiators told Boeing that it needed to come up with a better offer. Instead, Boeing tried to convince JetBlue to change the size of the airplane it was ordering. Ultimately, Neeleman decided to do business with Airbus on account of its superior offer and willingness to build the planes according to the specifications JetBlue wanted. Neeleman consummated the deal with a handshake. Then Neeleman telephoned Boeing to inform them.

"As soon as I called Boeing to tell them the deal was done," Neeleman said, "they wanted to reopen the deal. They wanted to give us the planes for the price we wanted."

Neeleman reminded Boeing that he had told them the rules up front. Boeing negotiators said they didn't know Neeleman was serious and as a result they had not given him their best and final offer. Boeing wanted a chance to submit a better offer.

Neeleman declined, citing his commitment to Airbus. "My word is my bond," Neeleman said. "I told you the deal is over."

Boeing countered that it could save JetBlue millions of dollars if Neeleman simply would allow them to submit a counteroffer.

"No thank you," Neeleman said.

Neeleman could have reopened talks with Boeing. He had not, after all, signed a contract with Airbus. He had given them a handshake. For Neeleman and the rest of the JetBlue management team, that was enough. "Our integrity was too important," Neeleman said. "Integrity is one of our five core values of the company."

When it was clear JetBlue would not entertain a better offer, Boeing requested an opportunity to send a team from Seattle to New York to meet with Neeleman to understand better what they did wrong in order to avoid making the same mistake next time around. Neeleman did not invite them to his office. He met them at the airport, listened to them, and then sent them on their way home.

This approach has paid off. "If things get tough and we need to get an airplane a little thinner or get some help on overhauling an engine," said Neeleman, "our suppliers like doing business with us and we are therefore able to do better deals with people who like and respect us. It is just the way we do business."

Opportunities to be dishonest in business present themselves every day, and none of these executives claim immunity from the pressures. "There is so much pressure to perform," said Dave Checketts. "Shareholders demand a certain kind of performance. You take that pressure, internalize it, and pass it down to other employees that work for you. They feel it and their job becomes 'How do we deliver to expectations?' instead of 'How do we do what is right?'"

Checketts acknowledged that part of this is structural. "In some companies, the entire management team has compensation incentives that are based on hitting the goals and expectations and achieving budgets," he said. "Thirty to forty percent of their livelihood is based on this. You get pressure from the top down to hit the mark."

To avoid these temptations, these leaders subscribe to some simple rules.

Rule #1: Stay Away from the Gray Zone.

As the chief financial officer for American Express, Gary Crittenden is ultimately responsible for the company's books and financial statements. Improper and dishonest corporate accounting practices have been the downfall of a parade of CFOs and CEOs at numerous high-profile companies over the past few years. The chief financial officers at Enron, Tyco, and WorldCom are just three of the more prominent ones to be indicted for dishonest accounting practices.

"Our approach isn't 'Should we book this or should we not book this?'" said Gary Crittenden. "Our approach is 'What's the right way to treat this?'"

As the CFO, Crittenden trains and instructs other accountants and finance executives at American Express. "I always say: 'If you ever see anything that's questionable, you need to raise it often enough and with enough people until you are absolutely satisfied you have the right answer.' That's just a hallmark. I don't mean to be Pollyannaish about it. That's just the way it is. We always ask the question in the first instance: 'What's the right thing to do?'"

Rule #2: Own the High Ground.

After taking over as CEO of Deloitte & Touche, Jim Quigley staked out seven strategic choices to frame the company's actions. Integrity is the accounting firm's first value. "I write and consistently reinforce in my speaking the importance of that value," said Quigley. "We have to own the high ground. What's important is that our employees know that's how I am. The employees need to know and understand that integrity is what this organization values."

This approach directly impacts how Quigley and his firm deal with clients. "When a client asks us to cut a corner, we won't do it," Quigley said. "If they push us unmercifully, we resign. We just walk away."

Rule #3: Make No Excuses.

The most important aspect of honesty in business is taking responsibility for one's own actions. In August of 2005, Dell Computers made an unusual announcement: It had fallen short of expectations and failed to meet its goals as well as the projections set by analysts during the second quarter of the year. Profits had gone up 28 percent that quarter. But overall Dell had expected revenues to rise by several hundred million dollars more.

Then Dell's CEO, Kevin Rollins, made an even more unusual announcement: He took personal responsibility for the shortfalls by blaming himself. In a conference call with reporters, Rollins said: "Frankly, we executed poorly on managing overall selling prices."

Following Rollins' announcement, the *New York Times* profiled his unusual management style, pointing out that "there's an established drill, or so it sometimes seems, when a publicly traded company disappoints Wall Street. The chief executive blames high oil prices. Or it's the fault of unforeseen happenings in Asia, or of a software upgrade that didn't go as planned."

The *Times* went on to say that Rollins "could have offered any number of excuses, not the least of which is Dell's own previous success. Its revenue grew 15 percent when compared with the same quarter last year—impressive for a company on target to bring in more than $50 billion in revenue over the next 12 months, but still short of its own expectations for an increase of 16 to 18 percent."

This wasn't the first time Rollins did this. In 2001 he blamed himself and fellow executives for failing to set the right tone. He said that the corporate culture at Dell had been tainted by greed. And he developed a new protocol that subjected every Dell manager—including himself—to periodic peer evaluations by subordinates. This generated some negative feedback about himself.

The ideal of taking responsibility when things go wrong sounds good on paper. But it can be very difficult to put into practice, especially for leaders in the limelight. The most difficult challenge of Dave Checketts' distinguished business career came when he violated his own rule about honesty.

During the NBA playoffs in 1999, the New York Knicks ran off a string of victories that would elate almost any sports executive. After barely qualifying for the playoffs, the Knicks upset the heavily favored Miami Heat in the first round. Next they swept the favored Atlanta Hawks. Then they earned a trip to the NBA Finals by miraculously beating Larry Bird's heavily favored Indiana Pacers, despite the Knicks playing without superstar center Patrick Ewing.

Knicks head coach Jeff Van Gundy had become the Little Engine That Could and New York fans were chanting "Jeff Van Gundy!" in the Garden. In the midst of this euphoric string of victories, Checketts got approached unexpectedly by a *New York Times* writer who said he had a story that Checketts had met with former Chicago Bulls coach Phil Jackson before the start of the playoffs. The suggestion was that Checketts had interviewed

Jackson about the prospect of replacing Van Gundy as the Knicks coach.

Checketts told the *Times* writer that it wasn't true.

Only it was true.

As the 1999 regular season wound down, the New York Knicks appeared to be in disarray. There had been infighting between coach Van Gundy and general manager Ernie Grunfeld, which resulted in Grunfeld being fired. Key players had injuries, and the team was playing far below expectations.

Meanwhile, Phil Jackson, the most coveted coach in the league, was available and Checketts had been told that the Knicks' cross-town rivals, the New Jersey Nets, were approaching Jackson. Checketts began preparations to make major changes in the organization if the team failed miserably in the playoffs. He invited Jackson and his agent to his home for an interview. The interview did not lead to a job offer and the Knicks far surpassed expectations in the playoffs.

"The team was doing so well and the city was alive," said Checketts. "It was such a Cinderella story about how these guys were playing so hard and overcoming injury. And the whole city was really behind Jeff Van Gundy."

Momentum in these situations is crucial. A news story reporting that Checketts had previously interviewed a replacement for Van Gundy might disrupt the team's focus and momentum. "The meeting [with Jackson] by itself wasn't a mistake," said Checketts. "Lying about it was. I had about two minutes to decide what to do. I should have said, 'I don't have to tell anybody who I meet with. It's not your business. I can just tell you I'm about making this club competitive and a winner. And I didn't like the way we were playing. But that's my only comment.'"

The night after he denied to the reporter his meeting with Jackson, Checketts could not sleep. "I wish I could take that moment back," said Checketts. "It was a mistake and I paid dearly for it."

After coach Phil Jackson confirmed he had in fact met with Checketts, a renowned columnist in the *New York Post* dubbed Checketts the Mormon Tabernacle Liar. "That was a dark hour," said Checketts. "I had set a standard for myself based on morals, principles, and ethics. When you violate those standards there are people waiting. It was an ugly time. There was a pile on."

Embarrassed and humiliated, Checketts faced another decision: whether to rationalize his behavior or accept full responsibility. He chose the latter. Checketts called a press conference, flatly admitted he had lied about the meeting, apologized to the *New York Times* reporter, took full responsibility for his actions, and vowed that a mistake like that would never occur again.

CHAPTER 6

TITHING COUNTS

Prior to becoming an executive at Dell, Kevin Rollins regularly attended all of Dell's board meetings as a Bain consultant assigned to the Dell account. At one particular board meeting Rollins made a presentation that predicted the company's stock price would increase dramatically.

Skeptical, one board member challenged Rollins. If Rollins was so confident, the board member asked, why didn't he go out and borrow millions of dollars and buy stock in Dell?

Rollins replied that he had enough money and didn't need a bunch more.

"It's never enough," the board member countered, dismissing the idea that a person could have enough money.

"I thought that was pretty sad," said Rollins. "It was never my goal to have infinite wealth. It's still not. It's not on my radar screen."

Greed is something Mormons are taught to shun. Dave Checketts didn't have to work very hard on this one as a youngster.

He grew up in a home without money. His mother mixed powdered milk with whole milk to make it stretch farther. Leftovers were eaten at the next meal. His mother harvested and canned peaches, pears, and garden vegetables to ensure they had food on the shelf during winter months. "Our family was always in financial trouble," said Checketts. "We'd be wondering if we would hang on to the house."

Today, Checketts owns two homes. He admits that living on the edge as a child and going without has given him added drive to obtain financial security as an adult. But he remains leery of greed. "Money or income doesn't buy happiness," said Checketts. "It never has. The greed will lead to other problems."

David Neeleman goes a step further. "I'm keenly aware that money can corrupt," Neeleman said. "I agonize over what effect money would have on my own kids and taking away their desire to work. So we made it clear to the kids that they won't be trust-fund babies. They've got to earn it themselves and make their own way. There are certain things we can help them with, which will still leave a lot of money to give away. We've toyed with the idea of setting up a charitable foundation and having the kids serve on the board. Together they could help give away money."

Money and the way these Mormon executives view the accumulation of personal wealth is influenced by the religious practice of paying tithing. The word *tithe* means "a tenth." While most churches collect donations from their members, the Mormon Church sets the contribution amount at 10 percent of all gross earnings. The practice of paying tithing stems from the Old Testament in the Bible. Eight years after Joseph Smith founded the Church of Jesus Christ of Latter-day Saints in 1830, he introduced tithing as a commandment. Mormons believe that God is the source of all blessings, spiritual and material. The principle behind tithing is that it teaches sacrifice and humility and affords individuals an opportunity to give back a percentage of what God has given them. The failure to pay tithing is like robbing God.

Combined, the CEOs in this book have earned hundreds of millions of dollars in cash and stocks. They have each paid tithing on all of their earnings. The practice is made easier by their perspective toward their money. "I don't think the ten percent is mine," said Kevin Rollins. "Frankly I don't think any of the money I make is mine. I just have the luck of having it to use, whether for good or not."

These CEOs' approach to tithing goes beyond just their annual salary. Kim Clark pays tithing on all capital gains; any gains realized through the sale of stock or real estate, all interest earned. "We try to put into practice the spirit of 'one-tenth of our increase,'" said Clark, who goes as far as to pay tithing on the imputed income from the special zero-interest mortgage that Harvard Business School holds on his home.

"Tithing conditions you that a certain percentage of what you make goes somewhere else," David Neeleman said. "It conditions you that it is not your money. It is a real valuable lesson. These are sacred funds."

The Mormon Church uses tithing funds to pay the cost of constructing churches and temples around the world. Thanks to tithing, no church buildings have a mortgage. Contributions from its members also enable the Church of Jesus Christ of Latter-day Saints to fund a vast worldwide relief effort. Whether working with the Red Cross to vaccinate 7 million children against measles in Mozambique, joining with Catholic Relief Services to airlift 40 tons of food to malnourished children in Niger, or sending truck convoys of food and supplies to hurricane victims in Louisiana, the Mormon Church uses the money from its members to help those in need around the world.

Although each of these executives makes plenty of money today, they began paying tithing when they had little. Gary and Cathy Crittenden bought their first home in the Boston area just after Gary finished his MBA at Harvard. The Crittendens were so cash strapped at the time that they cleaned out their savings and leveraged all of their limited assets to qualify for the mortgage and make the down payment. To cover the $3,000 in closing costs, they maxed out all their credit cards. For the following year they lived on a tight budget that included $600 in monthly living expenses for groceries, gas, utilities, and the mortgage payment.

One month Cathy withdrew $600 from the bank. Later that day she lost her wallet, which contained the entire withdrawal. It was never recovered. With virtually no cushion in their monthly budget, the Crittendens were in a bind with the loss of a month's living expenses. "We had to decide that month between paying tithing and paying some of our monthly expenses," Crittenden said.

They chose to pay tithing first. "From the time we were small we were taught that this is not our money to determine how it is spent," said Cathy Crittenden. "Not paying tithing has never been an option."

A few days later, an unexpected check arrived in the mail. The amount was almost identical to the amount the Crittendens had just paid in tithing. It was money owed to Crittenden for some previous side work he had forgotten about.

"You can say this was a coincidence," said Gary Crittenden.

"But it was an enormous blessing and it caused us to be more disciplined in the way we live. We try to live conservatively. We don't live high on the hog. All of that has been the influence of tithing."

NOT A SMALL THING

As a young boy, Kim Clark grew up watching his parents pay tithing every week. At the end of each year the family would meet with their bishop for what's known in the Mormon Church as *tithing settlement*, an end-of-the-year interview where families give a verbal accounting of whether they have truly given up 10 percent of their earnings to God through tithing. Unlike the IRS, the bishop doesn't ask for documentation or other proof. He simply takes the word of each family.

Clark had gone to tithing settlement with his parents and siblings since he was old enough to remember. These annual sessions were routinely no more than fifteen minutes in length and uneventful. His parents always paid an honest tithing.

One year, however, when Kim was about twelve years old, he accompanied his family to the end-of-the-year tithing interview and had an experience that changed forever his view toward tithing. Kim was seated across from the bishop's desk when the bishop said to Kim's father: "Well, Merlin, are you a full tithe payer?"

"No," Merlin replied.

Kim was stunned. So were his siblings. Kim's mother started to cry. His father did, too. The bishop was speechless. Not all Mormons are full tithe payers. But many are, and the Clarks had always strictly adhered to the principle of tithing.

Sensing that something bad had just happened, Kim listened

attentively as his father explained to the bishop that he and his wife had seen their finances stretched very thin. They had recently moved from Salt Lake City to another area due to Merlin's new job, but they had been unable to sell the Salt Lake home. With two mortgages, they chose not to pay tithing in order to keep the house. "But, Bishop, we will be full tithe payers in the future," Merlin promised.

The experience was humiliating for Merlin Clark. But it was a critical, formative experience for twelve-year-old Kim. "I learned what it feels like to sit and give an accounting to a bishop and say you are not a full tithe payer," he said. "I have never forgotten it and I never wanted to feel that way again."

A Mormon who does not pay tithing is not considered in good standing in the Church. Nonetheless, the Clarks' bishop did not chastise Merlin. Instead, he encouraged him to repent and return to paying tithing.

After leaving the bishop's office, the Clarks returned home and Merlin apologized to his children and vowed that he would never again fail to pay his tithing.

From that moment through his tenure as the dean at Harvard Business School, Kim Clark has always paid his tithing. "As a young boy I realized that while tithing may seem like a small thing, it is actually a huge thing in the economy of the Lord," Clark said. "It's huge because it springs from a really fundamental principle about the commitment you make when you covenant with the Lord, effectively that everything you have is his. Tithing is a principle that demonstrates that in fact you are committed to the basic idea that the earth is the Lord's and we are stewards only.

"So if you sit in the bishop's office and say you're not a full tithe payer, what you are really saying is: 'I'm not committed to the principle that the earth is the Lord's. I actually think that some of the earth is mine.' That's a big deal."

CORPORATE STEWARDSHIPS

This principle of stewardship was driven into Clark time and time again as a child. He heard stories of his great-great-grandfather Edward Bunker, who walked across the Plains five times and was sent on various missions by Brigham Young. Bunker was one of the Mormon pioneers who sacrificed everything to establish and build a foundation for future generations in Utah. "Why was he doing those things?" Clark asked. "He knew his responsibility was to build what he could build and that others would build on his foundation."

The principles of tithing and stewardship apply in Clark's work as dean of the Harvard Business School. "When you become part of an institution like the one I'm responsible for now," he said, "that principle of stewardship is deep in what I do; the sense that we are responsible for this institution for a time period. It's an important and good institution, one that can really improve things in the world. It has a good mission and a high purpose."

Under Clark's leadership, HBS has established five new research centers outside the United States, enabling Harvard to teach top business students in other parts of the world. It was part of Clark's vision to enable HBS to operate globally and become a more powerful institution throughout the world.

"The fact that I can establish research centers outside the U.S. depends critically on things that happened thirty years ago," Clark said. "The people who were running the school then are impacting what we do now."

Clark approaches virtually every decision he makes as dean with an eye toward how it will impact the next generation at the school.

"We have a legacy," he said. "We have a set of assets in this institution that was created by other people. We didn't build it. It was given to us. Now we are doing things that will down the road affect a lot of people. So I recognize that we are stewards at HBS. We have this for a time. It happens to be our time. It is our responsibility to do what we can in this time to make the institution as great, strong, and effective as it can be, and do things that will raise the foundation for what's coming."

"That logic or set of principles has been deeply engrained in me from an early day," Clark said. "I approach everything I do that way: my church, my work, and my family. There is a sense of building on things that have been done before us and preparing for others that will follow."

TITHING INSULATES AGAINST GREED

The *Wall Street Journal* reported in 2004 that the number of millionaires in the United States had surpassed 2 million and that the number of U.S. households with net worth of $5 million or more exceeded 1.2 million. The stock market rise in the previous decade and soaring executive compensation were cited as two explanations for rising personal wealth. The result has been a wave of luxury spending. "The rich are finding it harder to set themselves apart," the *Wall Street Journal* noted. "Many are turning to super sized luxury consumer products to rise above the pack." Examples include custom-built, super-sized yachts; luxury automobiles listing between $350,000 and $450,000 apiece; limited-edition wristwatches priced at $200,000; lavish vacation homes; racehorses going for up to $8 million; and pricey art. Sales of postwar and contemporary art by Sotheby's and Christie's exceeded $90 million in one month in 2004.

Mormon executives are generally quite frugal in their spending habits. "There's something about a lifestyle that demands sacrifice," Gary Crittenden said. "It makes you a happier person. Happiness doesn't come through self-indulgence."

An aversion to luxury spending has another benefit: It frees up these executives to focus more acutely on obligations to their companies and shareholders. The acquisition and maintenance of yachts, properties, and other luxury items can be a tremendous drain on a person's time. The more mental energy expended worrying over the protection of personal assets, the less energy is left for leading a company.

It also frees up more time to be with family. As JetBlue was preparing to go public, the investment bank handling the public offering sent Neeleman on a road show—a tour around the country to meet with potential investors. During the road show Neeleman traveled in private jets and private limousines, stayed in five-star hotels, and had a concierge person assigned to him at all times. All of this was paid for by the investment bank, which stood to make a lot of money by virtue of Neeleman and therefore wanted to keep him happy by essentially giving him whatever he wanted during the tour. The one thing Neeleman wanted most was to visit Salt Lake City in the midst of the road show in order to hear Gordon B. Hinckley, the prophet of the Mormon Church, speak at the Church's annual conference. The investment bank arranged for a private jet to take Neeleman to Salt Lake City, where he heard the prophet speak. In his message, the prophet said he was confident that when people stand before the judgment bar of God there will be little discussion as to a person's earthly wealth or earthly possessions. Rather, the conversations will dwell almost exclusively on a person's relationships, most particularly relationships with family members.

Neeleman took the prophet's words seriously. "I'm confident the Lord values the family above any other institution," said Neeleman, who jokes about how cheap he is when it comes to spending. The one thing he does spend money on is family vacations. He and his wife take their nine children on at least three family vacations each year. One time it may be skiing in Utah. The next time it may be Walt Disney World in Florida. But the spending is akin to investing in memories as opposed to accumulating monetary possessions.

David Neeleman has a very wealthy friend who has more money than he can spend. "He is constantly buying new things to make himself happy," Neeleman said. "Money and possessions don't bring happiness. Money can actually be a source of a lot of unhappiness." Time with family, on the other hand, brings lasting joy. And, relatively, it's pretty inexpensive.

Another primary reason Mormon executives focus less on luxury spending is that their faith teaches that successes, financial or otherwise, are blessings that come from God, and with that comes a duty to give back. "Tithing provides a very important context for how you think and act," said Jim Quigley. "When you pay tithing all you have to do is acknowledge that all these blessings come from God. He's asked for just a tiny, little piece back."

This perspective toward private assets carries over to the way these executives treat corporate assets. "As soon as you acknowledge that all that you enjoy comes from God," said Quigley, "you have overcome the Dennis Kozlowski effect."

On September 20, 2005, Tyco International's CEO, Dennis Kozlowski, and CFO, Mark Swartz, were sentenced to serve up to twenty-five years in prison after being convicted of twenty-two criminal charges pertaining to looting their former company. At the time these crimes occurred, Kozlowski and Swartz were two of the highest-paid executives at any American company. The court ordered them to pay $240 million in restitution and fines.

The trial of the Tyco executives revealed lavish corporate spending on personal luxuries, including a multimillion-dollar private apartment, artwork, and an overseas birthday party for the CEO's spouse. "He felt entitled to those things," Quigley said. "But a Mormon executive should not feel entitled to that because we don't think about the world's goods in the same context. One reason we don't see the world's goods in the same context is the principle of tithing."

As the CEO at Deloitte, Quigley has watched a series of other CEOs go to prison. Quigley personally made the decision to help MCI emerge from bankruptcy after its CEO, Bernard J. Ebbers, received a twenty-five-year prison sentence for masterminding a massive accounting fraud. He prepared a presentation titled "The New Age of Accountability" and stressed to his employees and his colleagues the need to avoid the three things that he believed led to these crimes: greed, entitlement, and rationalization. "Those are the underpinnings of excesses that were defined by the nineties," Quigley said. "People became greedy. They felt entitled to a certain share of the world's goods because they saw others who they didn't think were any more entitled to have such things. Therefore they rationalized errant behavior to get what they thought they were entitled to."

Perspective has a lot to do with why these executives pay

tithing. Their view toward money is not much different from their view toward any other commodity: It is perishable and not a true source of lasting joy. And most of these executives had experienced true joy and the practice of paying tithing at a time when they were without wealth. David and Vicki Neeleman have plenty of money now. They did not start out that way. When they got married, money was so tight that Vicki borrowed a wedding dress, served wedding guests a scoop of ice cream and a cookie for dessert, and went without a professional photographer. Vicki's high school photography teacher took wedding pictures. But even his pictures turned out to be too expensive, leaving the Neelemans to settle for snapshots taken by family members. "We had no money," Vicki Neeleman recalled.

The Neelemans' approach to money and tithing is no different today. "We remember humility," said Vicki Neeleman. "We remember the Lord is first, not us."

CHAPTER 7

THE TRAPPINGS OF POWER

In the spring of 2004, Kevin Rollins exited a vice presidents' meeting at Dell's corporate headquarters and was approached by Dell's founder and CEO, Michael Dell. At the time, Rollins was the company's president and he and Dell jointly ran the company. They did everything as a team. Even their offices were joined by doors that remained open virtually all the time. They referred to their management approach as "two in a box."

Rollins and Dell stepped into a private place.

"I'm thinking about having you be the CEO," Dell told Rollins.

The opportunity to be in charge of the most successful company of the 1990s would be a dream come true for most corporate executives. But Rollins never had his eye on the CEO title. First, he never thought Michael Dell would relinquish it. Second, Rollins wasn't sure he wanted to remain at Dell if Michael wasn't going to be around.

"Does this mean you are going to retire or do something else?" Rollins asked.

Dell assured him he was too young to retire and loved his company too much. He just wanted Rollins to be the CEO.

"If you stay involved," Rollins said, "I'd be happy to do it."

The pursuit of power is a motivating factor among some business executives. In the world of big business, titles and salary signify power. There is no greater title than CEO and chairman. Typically, no position is compensated more richly. But power and wealth often breed arrogance and are easily abused.

In his thirty-year career at Harvard Business School, Kim Clark has made some observations about power and those entrusted with titles such as CEO, president, or, in his own case, dean.

"When it comes to praise, if you are not careful you start imagining that people are talking about you personally, when they are in fact speaking about the organization," said Clark. "You can get yourself convinced that you are becoming really quite special. That's terrible. First, it's not true. Second, it is deadly to your spiritual well-being."

One of the most dangerous aspects of power that Clark sees is found in what he calls *the inner circle*. "Every organization has a group that you think of as the inner circle," said Clark. "That's the group that is in the know about what's really going on in the organization. It's where the important decisions are made that guide and direct the organization's affairs. It's where people assume power lies, where the general strategy and strength and power of an organization exist. The lure of the inner circle is in every organization."

Organizations create incentives to get people to do things that will advance them to the inner circle. These rights of passage often require demonstrations of competence, loyalty, and commitment to the organization. "Unless organizations are really careful, that can become really insidious in people's lives," said Clark. "One manifestation is a terrible thing called 'face time.' Instead of judging an individual on the basis of performance, we judge them on how often we see that individual around the office, especially at odd hours. If you are there at eight-thirty at night and on Sunday afternoons, you are obviously committed to the organization. So, independent of performance, the guys who get in the inner circle are the ones who are around the office a lot, getting face time with the key people."

One false impression of the inner circle is that a lot of the important work gets done not in the formal stuff, but in the informal networks. This inspires some to hang around the office more. "They are not doing anything productive," said Clark. "They just want to make sure people see them. It's insidious. That's how people lose their way.

"If the inner circle gets warped and you get lured in there, you're going to get warped, too. Very good people get twisted and begin to shade the truth, and change the records and engage in self-dealing. That's absolutely what happened at Enron and was a factor at companies like Tyco and WorldCom."

Clark insists that every organization has an inner circle. The nature of that inner circle depends on the personal priorities and leadership style of its members. "If the inner circle is strong and good and focused," said Clark, "they will judge you on performance, not face time. If the organization is twisted, you have to get out of that organization or you will get twisted, too."

The lure and prestige of the inner circle is one common trapping that comes with power. *Preferential treatment* is another.

"When you attain a certain position, people are not real with you," said Dave Checketts. "They want to gain favor. So they take care of everything for you if you let them. That's the first trapping of power."

This trap is particularly powerful in the entertainment industry. "In the entertainment business, everything you want you get," Checketts said. "It's very seductive. You feel like king of the world. It really does breed laziness and being out of touch. Plus you have so many resources at your command."

Deference is yet another trap associated with power. "When you're a leader you get treated differently," said Kevin Rollins. "People think you know a lot of things. And if you've got money, they treat you as if you know things you never even intended to know."

Preferential treatment and deference easily distort a leader's sense of self-importance. Manifestations of these trappings include private security personnel, limousines, preferred parking spaces, preferred seating, and individuals employed to insulate you from customers and employees. To remain grounded, Kevin Rollins has two mottos he lives by as a CEO.

1. You're Never as Important as You Think You Are.

Rollins chooses not to use a driver, preferring instead to drive himself to and from work each day. He refuses to use a preferred parking space at corporate headquarters. In fact, no Dell executive has a preferred parking space. Rollins does not use a corporate plane when flying on business for Dell; he uses his own personal plane. When he travels, he stays only in hotels he would stay in if he were footing the bill. Rollins even reads his own e-mail. "It's a very egalitarian work structure," said Rollins.

2. No One Is Irreplaceable.

"I realize there will be someone else who will run Dell when I'm not here," said Rollins. "They will forget about Kevin Rollins. It's just a fact. The same is true with being a bishop in the Mormon Church. The same is true with other civic responsibilities. The only place it is not true is in your family. Your kids don't forget that. No one will take the place of Dad, never."

David Neeleman doesn't use a personal driver either. Nor does he use a preferred parking space at JetBlue's corporate headquarters. Like Dell, JetBlue offers preferred space to none of its corporate executives. "All those trappings that come with being a CEO," said Neeleman, "I just don't like them."

This is evident in his office and in the way he interacts with his staff. Neeleman's office is not much bigger than his secretary's office space. They have the same industrial carpet. They have the same furniture—in fact, his secretary's may be a tad nicer. There is no expensive artwork or lavish furnishings. For lunch, Neeleman typically rushes through cold deli sandwiches while at his desk.

Jim Quigley runs the most powerful professional services firm in the United States. Yet his office also lacks lavish furnishings or extensive staff. The most outstanding objects in his office are extensive photographs of his wife, children, and grandchildren. They cover his desk, his bookshelves, and one wall.

For these guys there is no expensive art, no private elevator or personal security detail, no private dining room or butler. At Deloitte, Quigley has a simple rule: Don't Get Too Hung Up on Your Title.

"The key is not to allow your sense of who you are and your sense of self-worth to get tied up in your title," said Quigley. "Because when the title is gone you don't want to lose yourself."

One reason these Mormon CEOs have a different approach to power is the fact that most of them have also held leadership positions in the Church. In the Mormon faith, the greater the title the harder the Church expects the holder to work and serve his or her constituents. "As a bishop you are at the beck and call of every person in your congregation," explained American Express CFO Gary Crittenden, who has been a bishop. "Paradoxically, even though you are the leader, you really are the person who is responding to the needs of everyone else. Typically, people think of business leadership as being the exact opposite, that you sit in a room and tell people what you need and they bring it to you. But the model that you get from a bishop's perspective is that you are here to facilitate and serve others, to take roadblocks away for people who work for you in order to help them be successful. In a church setting, those roadblocks may be sin, an inability to live commandments, or a whole variety of personal issues. In a work setting, roadblocks can be insufficient talent, inadequate training, or the wrong person in the wrong job."

This approach tempers a bishop's outlook on power and titles. Crittenden compared a bishop's leadership to an inverted pyramid. "In business people think the base of the pyramid reports to the top and the top dictates what happens," Crittenden said. "In the Mormon Church it is the other way around. The top of the pyramid is actually the breadth of the Church and it reports down to the bishop, who is doing his best to keep everything going."

These Mormon CEOs view their job as facilitative as opposed to driving those people who work for them. "I'm a different CEO by virtue of the experiences that I've had that brought me here," said Quigley. "I have 2,600 U.S. partners and I want them empowered to act. I lead them in a principle-based way. I'm not trying to lead them in an organizational chart, where you report to me and I'm operating from a command-and-control approach."

The Mormon Church also expects its ecclesiastical leaders to build consensus. It is, after all, a volunteer or lay ministry. Quigley prefers this approach in his CEO role. "We agree on what we want to accomplish," he said. "We agree on how we are going to organize. Then they are empowered to act."

Another influence that being a bishop has on being a CEO pertains to how these corporate executives deal with employee disputes, insubordination, and the need to discipline or fire employees. "Great leaders relate to other people real well," said Kim Clark. "They have empathy. They can motivate and love people. The Mormon Church helps you do that. If you really like people and come to love them, you will make sacrifices and do things that help them succeed."

As the CEO of Madison Square Garden Corp., Dave Checketts made a point to take one road trip each year with the two teams owned by MSG: the Knicks and the Rangers. One year while traveling with the Rangers, Checketts was forced to make a difficult personnel decision. The Rangers were preparing to leave St. Louis after losing a game the previous night. Before boarding the team bus, Checketts was approached by the team's general manager and head coach. It was clear from their facial expressions that a problem existed.

They told Checketts that during the night, player Kevin Stevens ended up in one of the city's worst neighborhoods, where he was caught doing cocaine with a prostitute. The prostitute also had a gun. Stevens had been arrested and was being held at a jail in East St. Louis.

Angry, the Rangers head coach wanted to teach Stevens a lesson by leaving him behind in St. Louis. It wasn't the first time Stevens' substance abuse problems had landed him in trouble. The coach wanted to leave Stevens in jail to fend for himself.

"We're not running out on this guy," said Checketts. Bishops spend a great deal of time with people who are in trouble, people who are desperate. Before becoming a bishop, Checketts had also spent two years on his Mormon mission serving people who had spent time in the criminal justice system.

The Rangers coach kept pushing to leave Stevens in jail.

Checketts refused, insisting he was not going to leave a team member in jail in East St. Louis.

Checketts sent the team ahead to the next city it was due to play in. He headed to the jail, where he found Stevens in a crowded, primitive holding cell. He was barefoot, filthy, unshaven, and reeking. Checketts promised to get Stevens out of jail. But not before Stevens promised to accept treatment. "If you're not ready to do that then I'll leave you here," Checketts told him.

Before getting to Stevens, Checketts had telephoned Mrs. Stevens and told her what happened. Having endured previous incidents related to Stevens' substance abuse, she told Checketts she had had enough and was prepared to leave him.

Checketts conveyed this to Stevens in his cell. Sobbing, Stevens pleaded to see his children. "I understand," Checketts recalls telling him. "But these choices you are making are taking you further away from them. Fortunately, you are still alive."

Over the course of the day, Checketts spoke to Mrs. Stevens six times. He got a commitment from Stevens to enter treatment. When the judge set bail, Checketts paid it. Checketts didn't have the company's bottom line on his mind as he stood in the jail. Stevens had hit rock bottom. His chances of performing for his employer again were remote. "The lessons I learned on my mission had a lot to do with my approach to Kevin Stevens," said Checketts. "I couldn't leave him. He was so penitent anyway. He had been humbled beyond all belief. He had no shoes and was in jail."

At one time, Stevens was clean cut, a tremendous athlete with a beautiful wife and attractive, healthy children. Now he was facing the consequences of his addiction and possible long-term incarceration. "This is not about Kevin Stevens the player," Checketts told him. "This is about Kevin Stevens the person. I'm willing to get you out and get you going on the right path, but it's time to ignore hockey. This is about the rest of your life."

Kevin Stevens never played another game for the New York Rangers. Checketts did not renew his contract. But Checketts helped get him enrolled in a treatment program near Stevens' home in Connecticut. He remained in the program and remained married to his wife.

Insubordination sometimes requires stiffer actions. "You also have to make tough decisions," said Kim Clark. "Sometimes you have to reprove people or fire people who misbehave. You have to make tough decisions that hurt people. But you can do it in a way that recognizes you are dealing with human beings."

When situations call for it, each of these CEOs has demonstrated the ability to fire subordinates. "If someone gets out of bounds," said Jim Quigley, "they get corrected sharply and swiftly."

Dishonesty is the sort of thing that prompts Quigley to terminate an employee. "It's tragic," Quigley said. "But someone who isn't able to fill out an expense report truthfully cannot be allowed to sign my firm's name to financial statements. I'm not willing to trust that person professionally if I can't trust them to be honest in filling out their expense or time report."

Checketts has fired his share of employees, too. The toughest termination he ever handled involved one of his closest friends. After Cablevision Systems Corp. obtained ownership of Madison Square Garden Corp., Checketts remained the CEO of MSG Corp. But the Dolan family, which controls Cablevision, installed Marc Lustgarten as chairman of the board of directors, giving him oversight of all Cablevision's subsidiaries. In effect, Lustgarten became Checketts' new corporate boss. In 1999 Lustgarten told Checketts he had a choice to make: fire either head coach Jeff Van Gundy or general manager Ernie Grunfeld.

The timing could not have been worse. Only ten games remained in the regular season and the team was fighting for a chance to qualify for the playoffs. Checketts tried to convince Lustgarten that it was not essential for the coach and the general manager to get along in order for the team to win and suggested holding off on changes in coaching or management until after the season. Lustgarten countered by telling Checketts that if he wanted his continued support he better fire either the GM or the coach by the end of the week.

Checketts felt he had no choice but to fire somebody. He interviewed the players and the assistant coaches. It was clear from those discussions that both were committed to the head coach and held him in high regard. "They loved him as a coach," said Checketts. "So firing him made no sense at all."

From a personal standpoint, firing Van Gundy would have been easier. Checketts and he didn't particularly get along at the time and weren't social friends. On the other hand, Checketts and Grunfeld were very close friends. So were their wives. Yet he felt he had to fire Grunfeld. As general manager, he had no day-to-day contact with the players and his dismissal would have no immediate impact on the team or its performance on the court.

Checketts had fired many people during his tenure as chief executive at MSG Corp. The causes ranged from theft and embezzlement to sexual harassment. "In instances like that I did fire people swiftly because the situation required it," said Checketts.

But firing a personal friend essentially because a corporate superior demanded it was different. "I didn't want to call in a close friend at nine in the morning and say, 'Here's Joe, a security guard. He's going to escort you back to your office. Pack your things up and go.'"

Instead, Checketts decided to break the news to Grunfeld away from the office, in a private setting. He and Grunfeld had a standing weekly dinner appointment on their calendars. When they met for dinner later that week, Checketts recalled, he looked Grunfeld in the eye and said: "Ernie, this is not going to be our typical weekly dinner. It's going to be the end of your run at the Garden."

Checketts told him that the dispute with the head coach had gone too far. "At that time I couldn't tell him what had really happened, that I was being forced to do something against my will," said Checketts.

Grunfeld was floored by Checketts' announcement.

Checketts said he told Grunfeld he hated the position he was in and that firing him was the hardest thing he had ever done in business.

Grunfeld said he couldn't believe Checketts was going to do it. Both men teared up.

"Everybody has an end to their run," said Checketts, who told him the formal announcement would be made the following afternoon at four.

Checketts and Grunfeld spent the next two hours talking. Checketts assured him that he could take his time cleaning out his office and assured him that the team would fulfill Grunfeld's employment contract; he had three years remaining at $800,000 per year. He promised to recommend Grunfeld for a job anywhere else.

Immediately after the firing was announced to the press, the Knicks went on a run and won eight of their final ten games, enabling them to qualify for the playoffs. The national media credited Checketts for inspiring the team by shaking things up and firing Grunfeld. "I knew the winning had nothing to do with that," said Checketts. "But the press was saying, 'Look, he shook this place up.'"

Meanwhile, Grunfeld's wife complained to the press that her husband had been fired over dinner. This triggered critical stories about Checketts being ruthless and coldhearted. Then Checketts got a personal letter from Yankees owner George Steinbrenner, which complimented Checketts and told him that sometimes the loneliest place of all is that place reserved for a leader.

Another aspect of the Mormon religion that influences these CEOs' perspective toward power and titles is the Church's unique belief that families can be eternal. Mormons subscribe to the traditional Christian belief in resurrection or an afterlife. They also believe that families or family units remain intact in heaven. Mormon marriage ceremonies do not include the phrase "till death do you part." Rather, their marriages are performed "for time and all eternity."

"This belief is a reminder that my family and my relationship with my wife and children is more important and long-lasting than my career," said Kevin Rollins.

This perspective not only impacts how these CEOs exercise power and authority at work, it influences the way they handle them as a parent. "In parenting there is a fine line between being their friend and being their disciplinarian," said Neeleman. "You have to keep those two things separate. But you don't want your kids to hate you or fear you. So you really have to lay out the rules and insure that kids know where they stand. And when they cross over the line, you have to let them know it and how disappointed you are in them."

Neeleman's father never used corporal punishment or yelling. "He'd just let me know he was disappointed in me," said Neeleman. "I'd rather he had given me ten lashes than have him tell me I disappointed him. If your kids look up to you and know the rules and the consequences, then you'll have their respect. If you try to be too much of a friend, you can lose that."

Dave Checketts' approach to problems at home is the same approach he takes in business: *If it's a problem that can be resolved with money, it's not a problem.*

Checketts learned this rule of thumb from Bill Bain, the original founder of Bain Consulting. Early in his business career, Checketts worked directly for Bill Bain, who often repeated that rule. He applied it to business, family, and other problems. This approach and a sense of humor can be the difference between abuse of power and proper use of power. Checketts found that out when his sixteen-year-old daughter made a series of mistakes that resulted in significant damage to the Checketts' home.

Teenagers in the Mormon Church are expected to get up early

during the school year and attend seminary classes before school starts. One morning sixteen-year-old Katie Checketts was running late for seminary class when she hurried to the garage, started up the Chevy Tahoe, threw it into reverse—and rammed into the garage door that she had forgotten to open. Instead of going inside and reporting the accident to her mother, she pulled forward, hit the automatic door opener button, and raised the wooden door. As the door came up, the broken door destroyed the metal tracking, sending splintered boards and metal everywhere. Then she backed over the debris and left for seminary.

Checketts returned home from an out-of-town business trip later that day. He had undergone a particularly difficult week at work and arrived home in a bad mood. The first thing he saw was a heap of wood and overhead metal tracks lying in the garage. He burst into the house and demanded to know what had happened to the garage door.

The family assembled and his daughter recounted the story. Checketts could feel his blood boiling as he listened. His daughter and the other kids could see the anger in his eyes. Then he remembered Bill Bain's words: If it's a problem that can be solved with money, it's not a problem.

"Honey," Checketts said to his daughter, "it just occurred to me that when I took driver's ed many years ago, at no time did anybody ever say to me: 'Before you back out of the garage, open the door.' And I'm sure no one ever said it to you. Well, now you know."

There was a pause. Then the entire family burst out in laughter and cheers. The problem had gone away.

CHAPTER 8

FIRST THINGS FIRST

"If you let it, work will take all your time. It can absorb every aspect of your life. So I decided to bind it."

—Kim Clark, dean of the Harvard Business School

"There's a time and a place for everything. Therefore you can't do all things extremely well all the time. There's a time for family, a time for business, and a time for church."

—Kevin Rollins, CEO of Dell computers

Gary Crittenden has made a career out of overseeing finances for a range of name-brand American companies. He has been chief financial officer at Filene's Basement; Melville Corporation, a $14 billion parent company to CVS; Marshalls; Linens-N-Things; Bob's Stores; KB Toys; Sears Roebuck & Co., and Monsanto Company. When Monsanto merged with global pharmaceutical and agricultural giant Pharmacia, Crittenden led the integration process. Then he called it quits in early 2001.

Three months into early retirement he and his wife, Cathy, had sold their home in Chicago and were making plans to go on a full-time, non-compensated service mission for the Mormon

Church. Then he got a call from old friend Ken Chenault, who was about to be named the new CEO at American Express. Chenault and Crittenden had begun their business careers together over twenty-five years earlier at Bain & Company, where they worked as consultants and shared an office. They had remained friends ever since. Chenault asked Crittenden to join American Express as executive vice president and CFO. Crittenden accepted, deciding his church mission could wait until he got older and retired permanently.

Crittenden's duties at the world-leading financial services firm are vast. They include: (1) providing leadership to the company's finance group; (2) serving as key adviser on strategic and financial matters worldwide; and (3) representing American Express to investors, lenders, and rating agencies. His typical work day starts at 6:15 A.M., when he leaves his house in New Canaan, Connecticut, and commutes to his office at corporate headquarters in Lower Manhattan, arriving most days by 7:45. He leaves the office most evenings at 6:30 and arrives back home around 8:00. This amounts to fourteen hours per day, door-to-door, or seventy hours per week. Crittenden spends an additional five hours each Saturday working from his home office.

Crittenden's title in the Mormon Church is stake president, an assignment he received shortly after accepting the job at American Express and relocating to New Canaan, Connecticut. He has oversight of seven bishops and congregations in Fairfield County in Connecticut and parts of Westchester County in New York. His church duties are performed without compensation and occupy about fifteen hours per week of Crittenden's time.

But the titles Crittenden takes most seriously are those of husband and father. Those obligations have another set of time obligations each week.

The ability to maximize work performance while balancing family obligations is the challenge of every working professional. "Work is all about what you actually deliver and very little about just spending time," said Crittenden. "Just putting in time doesn't help you much. It's about figuring out what needs to be done and mobilizing a larger organization to make it happen. If you can do that you have a lot of flexibility in how you use your time. The better you do that over time, the more time and flexibility you have."

To fulfill his obligations to his family, his company, and his church, Crittenden follows some basic rules:

Rule #1: Do the most important things first.
Rule #2: Do the urgent things second.
Rule #3: Delegate the things that are urgent but unimportant.
Rule #4: Skip altogether the things that are unimportant and
        not urgent.

The trick, he said, is distinguishing between what's most important and what's urgent. "It will never be urgent to put Easter eggs in the yard with my grandson," Crittenden said. "But it can be very important. So the question is what are the truly important things that I want to achieve in life and how do I plan those into my calendar first to ensure those things get done? Then you have to deal with the urgent things that are important, typically because they arise at work."

Crittenden reserves an hour every Sunday night to review his calendar for the upcoming week. That's when he sorts out the important from the urgent. In this process he applies the general rules above to the three primary areas that demand his time: his family, his occupation, and his church.

Under family, he asks himself three questions:

1. What can I do this week to be the best son my father ever had?
2. What can I do this week to be the best father to my children?
3. What can I do this week to be the best husband I can be?

Although these items rank highest on Crittenden's priority list, putting family first typically requires the least amount of his time. "It doesn't require much time to have your kids think you are really focused on them," said Crittenden, whose three children are now grown and living far from home. "It can be a couple phone calls a week or sending them a gift you pick out for them on the Web."

Doing one thing for his father each week doesn't require a great amount of time either. "Do I send him a card?" said Crittenden, whose mother has passed away. "Do I invite him to lunch? Do I arrange for a fishing trip to Alaska together over the summer? Or do I simply call him?"

Crittenden often uses his commute time to act on these questions and maintain his long-distance relationships with his children and his father. Facing a ninety-minute drive each way from home to work, Crittenden hired a personal driver in order to free himself up to utilize the three-hour commute time. He devotes some of that time to American Express business. He also takes care of personal priorities. Using a laptop and a cell phone, he communicates with his family members via e-mail and telephone, or writes them personal letters and cards. He also uses the time to arrange family vacations and special trips with individual family members.

To insure time with his wife, Crittenden blocks out Friday nights on his calendar. During the week Crittenden sees his wife for only two hours a day, between 8:00 P.M., when he gets home, and 10:00 P.M., when they go to sleep. That's why he rarely makes an exception to the Friday night rule. And rarely do the Crittendens include other social friends in this Friday night outing. "We do things that are totally mindless," said Cathy Crittenden. "We go to a movie or dinner. We don't do a lot of social things with other couples because there are so many social obligations through work. So we spend our Friday evenings alone."

Something as simple as reserving three hours a week to be alone together can go a long way toward insuring that a marriage remains healthy and strong. "In thirty years these jobs are gone," said Cathy Crittenden. "Then the question is what do you have at the end of it? Hopefully, you have another thirty years to enjoy each other and your children."

After these items are input into the calendar, Crittenden turns to his occupation and asks two questions:

1. What is the most important thing I need to do as an employee this week?
2. What is the most important thing I need to do as a boss this week?

From the minute Crittenden arrives at his office each day to the moment he leaves, he is all business. He even eats breakfast at his desk. Most of the meetings he attends, phone conferences he leads, training sessions he conducts, and reports he has to file are known and scheduled into his calendar way in advance. The purpose of the Sunday night calendaring session at home is to ensure that his upcoming weekly schedule emphasizes the most important things first and minimizes his direct involvement in the urgent.

"There's a whole series of things that are urgent but unimportant," Crittenden said. "Those things I don't do. I try to get someone else to do them, or I delegate them off. You get an awful lot done by letting people know they have accountability back to you within a certain time frame. I'm a big believer in patterns and follow-up."

Last, Crittenden reviews his church obligations for the upcoming week and asks:

1. What is the most important thing I have to do in my church assignment this week?

Typically, Crittenden spends two hours every Saturday on church work, conducting a one-hour leadership meeting from 6:00 to 7:00 A.M., followed by one hour of interviews with local church leaders from 7:00 to 8:00 A.M. The rest of his Saturdays he typically reserves for American Express work from home and family time. On Sundays Crittenden devotes anywhere from six to ten hours to his church assignment. He spends another four or five hours per week conducting church business from his car during his commute to and from work. Most of that work is done by e-mail and cell phone.

KNOW WHEN TO SAY NO

Another key to prioritizing time commitments is knowing when to say no. "There are roles in life I'd love to fill but simply can't," Crittenden said. "I'd love to spend more time with my friends. But it just isn't my season in life right now to do that. I've got kids spread all over the country. By the time I make them feel the right way and let my wife know that I love and appreciate her, there just isn't enough time left to do this other stuff."

By following these rules and repeating this process every Sunday, Crittenden ensures that the most important priorities don't get crowded out or compromised on his calendar. "This sounds pretty programmed," Crittenden said. "But in order to get a lot done requires a lot of structure. My life is so structured that I literally know where I'm going to be most days between now and a year from now."

Crittenden's planning habits may seem extreme. But the demands on his time are extreme. Meeting them requires unusual self-discipline. "Gary is the most disciplined person I know," Cathy said. "He is very diligent, very dedicated, and really organized, almost to a fault."

Even with all this careful planning and prioritizing, Crittenden's overarching approach to his calendaring is flexibility. When a situation arises at work that requires him to spend more than the standard seventy-five hours he devotes to American Express each week, he does it. "There are times when we're about to spin off twenty percent of our business at American Express," he said. "I'm not a very good stake president for the Church during that process. There are also times when church can be incredibly demanding, like when we're getting ready for a youth conference and executing the conference. When that occurs I spend more time than usual on church duties."

For a decade Kim Clark held the most prestigious position in business education in America: dean of the Harvard Business

School. During his tenure he presided over unprecedented construction on the Harvard campus, a 20 percent growth in faculty, and a rise in the endowment from $550 million to $2.1 billion. He also led the effort to expand HBS's reach around the globe by opening research centers in other countries. Clark also has served as a director on the boards of various American companies. The way he manages his time was established long before he became dean, however.

Clark came to HBS as an assistant professor in the summer of 1978. He had graduated from Harvard University in 1974 and received a Ph.D. in economics from Harvard in June of 1978. In 1984 he became a full professor with tenure at HBS. He became dean of HBS in 1995.

During the same ten-year span that Clark graduated from Harvard University, earned a Ph.D. in economics, and obtained tenure status as a faculty member at HBS, he and his wife had seven children. "The children were born from 1974 to 1984, coinciding with the most stressful years in my career," he said.

Clark and his wife knew that if they didn't put some rules in place to govern time management, both Kim's job performance and the family would suffer. "We learned early in our marriage, as soon as kids started coming, that if you let it, work will take all your time," Clark said. "The problems are daunting and there is a lot to do; it can absorb every aspect of your life."

Rule #1: No Work at Night.

For Clark, nights begin at 6:30 P.M. As long as he had children living at home, he made a point to be home by 6:30. From then until his children went to bed he did not think about work. "I had to be engaged at home," he said. "That meant bathing kids before bed, changing diapers, reading bedtime stories, assisting with homework, cleaning up the kitchen, or whatever else needed to be done."

"Kim made very strict rules for himself," said his wife, Sue. "One was to be home for dinner every night. He traveled a lot and consulted for companies. But if he was in town, he always made sure he was home for dinner. And from six-thirty to bedtime he was with the family."

This doesn't mean Clark never worked at night. He did on occasion. If an exceptional situation arose or a work assignment required attention after office hours, he would work on it. But his general rule of thumb was to wait until his children were in bed.

Rule #2: No Work on the Weekends.

Avoiding work on Sunday is a staple belief within the Mormon faith and is discussed in depth in the next chapter. But the decision to avoid work on Saturdays is a personal one Clark made to suit his family situation. He wanted to be sure he had adequate time with his seven children.

Rule #3: Every Rule Has Its Exceptions.

Balancing the time demands among work, family, and church is hard and requires flexibility. "There are times when I work at night or on a Saturday," Clark said. "But I try very hard not to violate these rules. It's not easy. I do it imperfectly. And it's not right to pretend there is a magic solution."

To enable him to follow these rules, Clark reorganized the way he spent his time at work. "In the office I realized that the number of hours I put in was not a good indicator of my output and my performance," he said. "What really mattered was being able to create high-quality production time." Before becoming dean at HBS, Clark devised three rules to enhance his productivity and efficiency at work dramatically.

Rule #1: Don't Talk to Anyone Before Noon.

Realizing that he performed at his peak in the morning, Clark made sure he was in his office no later than 7:00 A.M. each day. He would shut his door and work uninterrupted until noon. That meant his secretary didn't schedule any meetings or appointments during that time. Nor did she forward phone calls or messages. The only exceptions were if Clark's wife or the dean called. "I didn't talk to anyone before noon," Clark said.

The sustained, uninterrupted five-hour period proved far more productive than a ten-hour period filled with interruptions, meetings, phone calls, e-mails, and appointments.

Many professionals and business executives don't have the luxury of going without meetings, phone calls, or e-mails from 7:00 A.M. to noon each day. Nor was Clark able to maintain this practice once he became dean—the demands of leadership and the minute-to-minute changes in a schedule that can come with an executive position require more flexibility. But the principle of reserving a certain amount of time each day where Clark avoids e-mails, phone calls, and meetings remains part of his routine.

Rule #2: Schedule All Meetings and Interactions with Staff in the Afternoon.

At noon Clark would open his office door and keep it open until sometime after four. During this time slot he would hold all of his meetings, interact with staff and other faculty, and take and make phone calls.

Rule #3: Plan the Next Day Before Going Home.

At the end of the day Clark would shut his door, review what he accomplished during the day, and map out what he needed to do the next day. "Then I'd pack up and go home and leave it behind," he said. "I'd reserve the evenings for family and church. Then I'd get up early in the morning and crank away again."

After twenty years of cranking away under those rules, Clark was named dean at HBS. By then some of his children had married and Clark would soon become a grandfather. The change in his family situation and the new demands of being dean caused him to modify his schedule and time management rules. "In my life now I do four things," he said. "One is work, being the dean. That job has so many dimensions to it. Second is my family. That means everything from spending time with my wife to baby-sitting grandchildren. Three is church. Fourth is golf, my only big hobby."

For ten years Clark has held the dean's post at HBS. During that time he continued to maintain strict time management rules. "The rules have to do with putting some boundaries on work," he said. "We learned early in our marriage that work, especially the kind of stuff I was doing, if you let it would take all my time, every hour of every day. So we decided we had to bind it. The rules are simple and powerful and I still use them today. I've done it for thirty years."

Under this approach, Clark averages fifty-five to sixty hours in the office per week. But about a third of that—twenty to thirty hours—is what Clark refers to as the "critical" time, when he works without distractions.

*   *   *

Kevin Rollins, the CEO of Dell, takes a different approach to scheduling. The corporate culture at Dell and the duties Rollins has as its leader demand a more nimble approach to time management. "I'm not one of those who say you balance it all out and that you are home every night," said Rollins. "No, sometimes I'm gone all the time due to business obligations."

On average, Rollins works eight to ten hours a day. His daily schedule includes time for physical exercise and reading—he reads three to four books at one time. To ensure time for family and religion, Rollins seldom works Saturdays, never works Sundays, and reserves Monday nights to spend time with his wife. "I'm very dedicated to holding those times aside as sacred for those needs," he said.

Nor does he bring work home. "I'm a firm believer that there is a time and a place for everything," Rollins said. "Therefore, you can't do all things extremely well all the time. There's a time for family, a time for business, and a time for church."

When Rollins is at work, his focus is intense, uncompromised, and entirely on Dell. And with Dell extending its global reach into foreign markets, Rollins maintains a heavy travel schedule that sometimes requires him to fly on Sundays and keeps him away from home and church obligations for extended periods of time. "Sometimes the Church or church assignments get postponed," Rollins said. "But then when I'm home sometimes the business suffers. That's how you balance—you don't try to do too many things all the time."

The demands of running a large company can easily eat up any potential family time. Even when executives are home, it's difficult not to bring their work with them, particularly in times of crisis. One of the most difficult and stressful points in Rod Hawes' career came right after he and his partners purchased control of an insurance company in Tampa, Florida. Only after acquiring it did

Hawes discover that the company's balance sheet had severe deficiencies. Millions of shareholders' dollars were at risk. Hawes immediately put his house on the market in Connecticut, moved his family to Tampa, and took over as CEO of the company. For the next few months his family hardly saw him as he tried to navigate the firm through the financial crisis.

On one particularly bad day among a string of tough weeks at the office, Rod arrived home much earlier than usual. That and the look on his face as he walked through the front door told his wife, Beverly, that a major financial fiasco had occurred.

"What's wrong?" she asked.

Silent, Rod dropped his briefcase on the sofa and removed his suit jacket, tie, and shoes. Then he walked past the children, out the back door, and to the pool. Fully clothed, he jumped in.

Beverly couldn't believe it. The kids loved it. Convinced their father was playing a game, some of them jumped in before bothering to change into their bathing suits, too. Beverly couldn't help but laugh. After about five minutes, Rod emerged from the pool with a smile. "I am having a mid-life crisis and that is all the time I had to give it," he told her. Then he went off to his bedroom to change his clothes.

"Everybody had a good laugh," Beverly recalled. "And that's exactly what he needed."

Each of these men has a different approach to achieving the same objective: maximizing his time and output in the business world while maintaining a strong time commitment to family and church. "It's not right to pretend there is a magical solution," said Kim Clark. "I'm not perfect and it's not easy. The key is to establish some rules and try very hard not to violate them. The rules have to do with putting some boundaries on work."

CHAPTER 9

A DAY OF REST

"I maintain you'll never get fired because you weren't there on Sunday."

—Dave Checketts, former CEO of Madison Square Garden

"The principle of not working on Sundays doesn't mean you never travel on Sunday to get to a business meeting somewhere on Monday morning, or tend to urgent matters. Company employees are 'family.' And if there are emergencies or circumstances that require attention on Sunday, when you are a CEO of a large corporation you must make yourself available and respond just as you would for your personal family members."

—Rod Hawes, former CEO of Life Re

"In all these situations you have to do what you think is best. If there is a crisis, I would be there for my people."

—David Neeleman, CEO of JetBlue Airways

In 1998, Disney CEO Michael Eisner summoned Dave Checketts to a meeting at Disney's corporate headquarters in Los Angeles. At the time Disney owned two professional sports franchises: Major League Baseball's Anaheim Angels and the National Hockey

League's Mighty Ducks. Disney hoped to sell both. But first Eisner wanted to turn both clubs into winners in order to drive up their value.

The job was a dream job in many respects. But during the interview, Checketts noticed a big sign behind Eisner's desk that read: IF YOU'RE NOT HERE ON SATURDAY, DON'T BOTHER TO COME IN ON SUNDAY.

Checketts knew he had a problem. "You know what, Mike," he recalled saying to Eisner. "It probably won't work for me because I've got to have one day that I can dedicate to my kids and my church. It's just too important to me. If I don't have that kind of family time on the weekends, I assure you I will be miserable. Then we both lose because you won't get the results you are looking for."

One of the cardinal commandments of the Mormon Church is keeping the Sabbath day holy. The chief aspect of this commandment is to treat Sunday as a day of rest from labor and dedicate the day to family, worship, and service to others.

Before being named president of the New York Knicks, Checketts was president of the Utah Jazz, another NBA franchise. NBA teams often play games on Sundays. Checketts, who was serving as a bishop in a congregation of over 700 people in Salt Lake City, made a habit of trying not to work on Sundays. He brought this approach to New York when the Knicks organization hired him as the president and general manager in 1991. At the outset, Checketts informed his superiors and the people who worked under him that he didn't work Sundays. "I made clear to everyone that I was not going to be there on Sunday," Checketts said. "That's the way that it is. Sunday is a family day for me. It's a rest day. It's the one day I have to recharge my batteries. I wasn't going to leave home to go to work on Sunday."

After ITT and Cablevision Systems paid $1 billion to acquire Madison Square Garden Corp., Checketts was elevated to president and chief executive. In his new role, he had oversight of Madison Square Garden, its subsidiary companies the New York Knicks and the New York Rangers hockey franchise, and the Garden's MSG television network.

With his expanded corporate duties, Checketts had responsibility for all entertainment and events held in the Garden's various facilities. An event was scheduled for every Sunday of the year. Yet Checketts largely stuck to his no-work-on-Sundays routine, meaning he did not go to the office or hold meetings, negotiations, or planning sessions on Sundays. But on a handful of occasions during his eleven-year tenure at MSG, he attended Sunday games and special events, such as a memorial service held at the Garden for Israel's Prime Minister Yitzhak Rabin after his death in November of 1995.

"I work very hard," Checketts said. "But not on Sunday. It doesn't mean you can't take a phone call or send an e-mail on Sunday. But work will overcome you. It will control your life unless you give it some boundaries. It's like everything else; it has to have some boundaries."

Devoting Sundays to family and church enabled Checketts to maintain a torrid work pace during the rest of the week. On most days he left home in New Canaan, Connecticut, at 6:30 A.M. to commute to New York by car. He began working the moment his driver picked him up. Checketts converted the car to a mobile office, specially outfitting it with a television and VCR, enabling him to review game film and MSG Network productions while in transit.

He was typically the first one in the office and he would often not return home until 11:00 P.M. each night. Some nights he didn't come home at all. His business obligations frequently required him to attend late dinners and late-night meetings in the city, as well as night home games and other performances at Madison Square Garden. On some occasions he stayed at a Midtown hotel, where he maintained a home away from home. "I could have been gone every night," Checketts said. "Instead, I limited it to two nights away from home per week."

The only break he'd take from business each day was a self-imposed, mandatory one-hour exercise routine every afternoon at five o'clock.

He kept up this pace for eleven years. During this time he and his wife raised six children. On top of that, Checketts served as the youth leader to all the teenage boys in the Mormon Church congregation in New Canaan, Connecticut. Besides attending three hours of church services each Sunday, all Mormon teenagers are expected to participate in daily seminary or scripture study, as well as attend one weeknight activity each week to be trained in leadership and personal responsibility. The administration and oversight of the youth program is considered one of the most important and time-consuming responsibilities in the Mormon Church.

Under Checketts' leadership, Madison Square Garden thrived commercially and its sports teams excelled. The *New York Times* described Checketts as the one who "revved the engine and drove the car that roared down Broadway . . . the man behind the Garden's renaissance." During his tenure, Checketts led the effort to purchase and refurbish Radio City Music Hall. The Knicks reached the NBA Finals twice. The Rangers won a Stanley Cup championship. And the Garden achieved record financial performance and grew cash flow in double digits every year of his tenure.

This all occurred with the chief executive rarely working on Sundays. "I maintain you'll never get fired because you weren't there on Sunday," Checketts said.

All of the Mormon business leaders in this book have a general rule against working on Sundays. They all try to avoid it. But strict adherence to this principle is easier for some than for others. Running Harvard Business School presents fewer challenges to this habit than running a worldwide computer company such as Dell, or being the CFO of American Express. These positions sometimes require travel on a Sunday in order to get to business meetings somewhere else in the country or the world on Monday morning.

Some Mormon principles, such as integrity, tithing, fidelity to your spouse, and avoiding alcohol and tobacco, are non-negotiable. There is never a time when it is appropriate to break these principles. Yet there are circumstances when exceptions are made to travel on Sunday for business or when it becomes necessary to attend to business obligations on a Sunday. The aim of each of these executives is to treat Sundays as a sacred day for worship and family. But they do what is necessary to ensure that they are not shirking their professional obligations to employees and shareholders.

"This is a practical approach to business," said Rod Hawes, former CEO of Life Re. "When I went to Harvard Business School I never studied on Sundays. That was family time and church time. And by devoting that time to family I was refreshed on Monday morning and performed better during the week. When you don't have a break it wears you down."

Hawes found that his approach to avoiding studies on Sunday worked in a business setting, too. "You need time off on Sundays to really focus on family and refresh yourself," he said.

Since he tried to avoid work on Sundays as a CEO, Hawes never required his employees to work Sundays, either. "It's good for people who work for you to know they are encouraged and even expected to take personal time, too."

Hawes had the kind of business that enabled him and his employees to remain closed on Sundays. That is not the case for most of the CEOs in this book. Airlines, food and grain production companies, and financial services firms with a presence around the globe must operate on Sundays. And as the CEOs of those firms, these men respond to situations that occasionally require them to engage on Sundays. "The principle of not working on Sundays doesn't mean you never travel on Sunday to get to a business meeting somewhere on Monday morning, or tend to urgent matters," Hawes said. "Company employees are 'family.' And if there are emergencies or circumstances that require attention on Sunday, when you are a CEO of a large corporation you must make yourself available and respond just as you would for your personal family members."

JetBlue CEO David Neeleman doesn't work on Sundays, for example. But he makes himself available to his crew members if situations call for it. "In all these situations you have to do what you think is best," Neeleman said. "If there is a crisis, I would be there for my people."

During the Thanksgiving weekend holiday in 2004, the Neeleman family flew on JetBlue from New York City to Salt Lake City to be with family. The return flight put them in New York City on a Sunday afternoon. The Sunday following Thanksgiving is the busiest air travel day of the year for JetBlue and most airlines. When his flight touched down in New York, Neeleman saw that his flight crews were stretched to the limit. He decided to go to work.

As a result of the flight schedule, the family had already missed church services in Connecticut. With the children tired, Neeleman put his family in a car and sent them home to sleep. He remained at the airport for the rest of the day working alongside his crew members. He unloaded baggage from airplanes, tagged bags, pulled tickets at the gate, and cleaned airplanes.

On the busiest travel day, his employees needed extra support. As the leader of the company, Neeleman felt an obligation to be there and work alongside them.

All these executives have rules for time management. For the most part, these rules are based on principles. But the guiding theme for each of these rules is flexibility. "The honest answer is that you don't do it evenly all the time," said American Express CFO Gary Crittenden. "You expand and contract based on the situation, and you hope over time that the theme you are playing toward is one of these important areas and that you are not dropping the ball in the things that are really important. For me, I expand and contract a lot."

CHAPTER 10

WHAT MATTERS MOST IS WHAT LASTS LONGEST

"Sometimes in the business climate it is easy to get things backward and start thinking that business is more important than the family."
—David Neeleman, CEO of JetBlue Airways

The Mormon faith puts family and God above work in terms of importance. But imbedded in the Mormon faith is a high premium on hard work and exceptional performance in the workplace. The Church also teaches that the best way to serve God is to serve your family. One way to serve family is to work hard for an employer, enabling one to provide for the family. As a result, Mormons are taught that church obligations should not come at the expense of family priorities or professional obligations.

At the foundation of this approach is the underlying belief that no success can compensate for failure in the home. "Family has to come before everything else," said Dave Checketts, who logged fifteen-to-eighteen-hour days, six days a week, for nearly eleven years while at the helm of Madison Square Garden and the New York Knicks. Although his time was largely consumed by work, his approach to the family indicated that family remained his top priority.

"If my children call me during the day and leave a message, I return those calls first, not last," Checketts said. "I have had to run out of meetings and run out of critical situations to make my children a priority."

One of those situations occurred in May of 2001, on Checketts' last official day as CEO at Madison Square Garden. Checketts was in Long Island at the headquarters for Cablevision, Madison Square Garden's parent company. Tension between Checketts and Cablevision chairman Jim Dolan had been mounting for weeks, and their meeting in Dolan's office had reached a difficult point when Checketts' personal assistant entered the room and told Checketts he had an urgent call from his teenaged son.

"Dad, Winston is dead," his son told him.

Winston had been the family dog for over fifteen years. Part husky and part golden retriever, Winston had been the most loyal and gentle friend Checketts and his children had ever known. He was family.

Besides Checketts' daughter Elizabeth, three of the younger boys were home alone with Winston. Debbie Checketts was away.

Checketts hung up and turned to Dolan.

"Jim, I'm going home."

"You can't leave now," Dolan shouted.

Checketts told him he had to; his sons needed him. He did not tell Dolan why.

When he pulled into his driveway, he spotted his three sons sobbing and huddled around a blanket they had placed over the dog on the front lawn.

Checketts went inside and changed out of his business suit. He checked his home voice mail. It contained a series of messages from Dolan, all of which were marked urgent and said: "Call me." Checketts ignored them. Instead, he retrieved shovels and he and his boys dug a six-foot-deep hole for Winston.

He and his sons placed Winston in the grave. Then each of them placed in the grave one personal item that said something about the dog. They sobbed as they outlined what they had chosen to put in the grave. The boys chose to bury some of their most personal possessions. Then they buried Winston.

"If I had missed that time with those boys and had not been there for Elizabeth, that would have been truly tragic," said Checketts. "It wasn't a tragedy to leave an eleven-year business venture. But had I missed my sons and my daughter coming to the end of an era in our family that would have truly been tragic. It is an evening I will never forget.

"I'm hoping the one thing my children will say about me is that even though I worked very hard and was involved in a lot of things, there will be no question in their minds that they were first, regardless of when or where. That's how my parents treated me."

Running Dell is a lot different from running Madison Square Garden. But Kevin Rollins shares the same perspective as Dave Checketts. "I realize that there will be someone else who will run Dell when I'm not there anymore," Rollins said. "They will forget about Kevin Rollins. It's just a fact. The same is true being a bishop in the Mormon Church or holding a position of civic responsibility. No one is irreplaceable. The only place this is not true is in your family. Your kids and your loved ones don't forget that. No one will take the place of Dad, never."

The Mormon Church teaches its members that the family is

the fundamental unit of society and that nothing is more critically connected to happiness. The Church's family-centered perspective encourages mothers and fathers to strive to be among the best parents in the world. Teachings and programs are geared to aid parents in this quest and are sometimes referred to by church leaders as the "scaffolding" that helps build the individual and the family. Church leaders have gone as far as to publish a proclamation on the family in 1995 that declared: "Husband and wife have a solemn responsibility to love and care for each other and for their children."

Frequently traveling overseas for Dell, Rollins goes to extraordinary lengths to fulfill his parental duties at home. He will routinely call home in the evening to help his youngest son with homework. On one occasion Rollins was in Asia, where the time difference with Texas was fourteen hours. His son was struggling with some math assignments. Rollins called home to work through the assignments with him during his son's regular homework hour. That required Rollins to be up at 4:00 A.M. his time. "He had flown the previous day across the world," recalled Debbie Rollins. "He didn't care about the fact that he should have been sleeping or that it was so costly to make an hour-long phone call from Asia to home. The kids never feel like they are missing their father."

It's easy to see how some might think such a strong commitment to family might compromise performance or productivity at work. These leaders have found just the opposite: A strong family commitment enhances performance and optimizes productivity on the job. "I've seen a lot of people that have neglected their families," said David Neeleman, "and then they are not productive at work because they are so preoccupied with family problems that it negatively impacts their ability to complete their assignments at work."

One of Neeleman's highest priorities at work is productivity and efficiency. He expects it from his employees. He demands it of himself. "There are a lot of people who are a mess at work when they are not right at home," said Neeleman. "If things are right at home, you're more productive at work."

In the spring of 2005 JetBlue was actively raising more money from investors. As CEO, Neeleman went on a national road show—a tour to meet with investors, show off the company's strengths, and sell investors on the idea that the airline is a good investment. One week into the tour Neeleman had scheduled appearances in Milwaukee, Kansas City, and Chicago. In the midst of the trip Neeleman received a call from home informing him that his son's high school lacrosse team had just won a critical game and would therefore be playing a playoff game on the same day Neeleman would be meeting with investors in Kansas City. "I called the investors in Kansas City and said, 'Let's schedule for another day; I really want to go to my son's lacrosse game.'"

The investors understood. One even commented on how much he liked that approach and would do the same thing in the same situation. The meeting was rescheduled. Neeleman flew home and saw his son's game and then later returned to Kansas City.

Neeleman regularly jams his schedule in a manner that requires him to move around the country at a whirlwind pace in order to ensure that he doesn't miss events with his children. In June 2005, Neeleman flew to Orlando, Florida, where he joined Florida governor Jeb Bush for a ribbon-cutting ceremony at Jet-Blue's new $25 million training facility near the Orlando airport.

David Neeleman while on a mission for the Mormon Church in Brazil. He spent two years in some of Brazil's most poverty-stricken villages and learned to speak Portuguese fluently.

David Neeleman and his wife, Vicki, have nine children. The family moved from Salt Lake City to Connecticut to launch JetBlue.

Dave Checketts (right) honors David Neeleman, a close friend and fellow member of the Mormon congregation in New Canaan, Connecticut, with an award for public service at a New York event.

After running the Utah Jazz and working in the NBA Commissioner's Office, Dave Checketts (seen here with former New York City mayor Rudy Giuliani and NBA Commissioner David Stern) became president of the New York Knicks in 1991.

After Dave Checketts became president of the New York Knicks he promptly hired Pat Riley (center) as head coach. Former Knicks GM Ernie Grunfeld is on the right.

Dave and Debbie Checketts have six children, three of whom are married.

Clayton Christensen (shown here with his wife and children) was a Rhodes Scholar at Oxford and White House fellow before joining the Harvard Business

Clayton Christensen currently serves as a business consultant to Intel, Kodak, Eli Lilly, and Dell.

Harvard Business School professor Clayton Christensen spent two years in Korea as a missionary for the Mormon Church.

Before obtaining his doctorate in economics from Harvard, Kim Clark served a mission for the Mormon Church in Germany. At age nineteen he served as financial secretary to the mission president, learning valuable lessons about management, budgeting, financial oversight, and organization.

As the dean of the Harvard Business School from 1994 through 2005, Kim Clark (seen here dedicating the Spangler Center on the HBS campus in January of 2001) presided over a $10 billion endowment.

Kim Clark and his wife, Sue, have seven children and six grandchildren.

Jim and Bonnie Quigley (center) have three children and nine grandchildren. On 9/11 Quigley led the evacuation of more than 3,000 Deloitte & Touche employees from the firm's headquarters at the World Trade Center complex.

Jim Quigley (#17) was born and raised in the rural town of Millar, Utah. In 1968 he quarterbacked his high-school football team to the state championship game.

Jim Quigley is the CEO of Deloitte & Touche USA, the nation's largest professional services firm. Aside from running Deloitte, he's a bishop in the Mormon Church, presiding over a congregation of 500 members in New Canaan, Connecticut.

COURTESY OF ALISON WACHSTEIN © 2006

Rod and Beverly Hawes (center) have six children and twenty grandchildren. "We know that family is the secret to happiness," says Beverly. "The things that happen in the business world are very important . . . but the things that happen at home have eternal significance."

COURTESY OF ALISON WACHSTEIN © 2006

Rod Hawes grew up in Marsing, Idaho, a ranching community with 400 residents. After becoming a Baker Scholar at the Harvard Business School, he co-founded Life Re Corp., the world's largest privately held life reinsurance company.

COURTESY OF JETBLUE AIRWAYS CORPORATION

In 1999 at age 37, David Neeleman raised $130 million in venture capital to start JetBlue, despite having no airline certificate, no planes, and no deal with the New York/New Jersey Port Authority. JetBlue now employs 17,000 employees and operates 340 daily flights in and out of 33 cities.

At age nineteen, Kevin Rollins served a mission for the Mormon Church in Alberta, Canada. "A mission teaches you to get up, get going and do things," Rollins says. "I also learned on a mission that if you just work really hard you'll get good results. But if you're smart and work really hard, you'll get superb results."

Michael Dell (left) asked Rollins to join his company as an executive in 1996. While assuming this new corporate responsibility, Rollins also served as a bishop for the Mormon Church, leading a large congregation in the Boston area.

After serving as chief financial officer at Sears, Roebuck & Co., Filene's Basement, and Monsanto Company, Gary Crittenden retired in early 2001 and began making plans to serve a full-time, non-compensated service mission with his wife for the Mormon Church. Then he got a call from American Express CEO Ken Chenault, asking him to join the credit card company as CFO.

During a mission for the Mormon Church in Germany, Gary Crittenden had a harrowing experience: In the dead of winter he fell into a deep well, crashing through a layer of ice and becoming completely submerged in freezing water. He fought his way to the surface and climbed out, despite wearing a suit and trench coat.

As soon as the ceremony concluded, Neeleman hustled back to the airport and boarded a flight to New York. After landing he drove himself to JetBlue's offices in Darien, Connecticut. En route he did business via cell phone. Once at Darien he held a one-hour meeting and then scooted to a nearby high school to watch his son compete in an athletic event.

"Sometimes in the business climate it is easy to get things backward and start thinking that business is more important than the family," said Neeleman.

The same week Neeleman opened JetBlue's new training facility with Governor Bush in Florida, Kevin Rollins flew to Brazil to represent Dell at a conference for corporate chief financial officers. He left Austin, Texas, on a Wednesday, flying all night to Brazil. He worked in Brazil all day Thursday and Friday. Rather than flying back at a more traditional flight time on Saturday or Sunday, or spending an additional day in Brazil to relax, Rollins went straight to the airport the moment his work was complete on Friday afternoon. Then he took an all-night flight back to Texas, arriving home Saturday just in time to attend his daughter's birthday party and her high school graduation party.

"I flew all night to get back," Rollins said. "So what? We're in a family. I flew all night because my daughter had a birthday. That's what we do."

Rollins routinely arranges his travel schedule in order to be present for his children's music recitals, school performances, and special occasions. And when he's not on the road, he builds in time to be with his kids as needed. "These things with family and not missing events don't show up as dramatic," he said, referring to the fact that his children just expect it. "I live a very scheduled life and these things are just planned in."

Getting to children's events is by no means easy and can require extraordinary scheduling maneuvers. Not everyone has the resources at their disposal to fly from one place to another to see a child perform in a high school sporting event. But the principle of putting kids first and making them feel important doesn't require being at every game or recital. After one of Kim Clark's sons graduated from high school and was preparing to leave home to serve his Mormon mission, he spoke in a church service about his deep love for his father. In doing so he talked about how his father attended every one of his games. "In reality," said Sue Clark, "I was the one at every game and Kim came when he could. But our son's memory is that his father was always there."

Another way these leaders remain involved with their children is to take their children with them on the road. Kevin Rollins makes a habit of taking his children with him on business trips as often as possible. "He prefers to have us with him when he travels," said Debbie. "That way when he's away he's not away from us." When appropriate, the Rollinses have even taken their children out of school to go on these business trips. For example, when Rollins had to spend an extended period in China, he took his entire family in the midst of the school year. "We took them to see the Great Wall," said Debbie. "The school was very supportive. Seeing the Wall rather than just reading about it was much more educational."

Harvard Business School professor Clayton Christensen published the best-selling book *The Innovator's Dilemma*. It examined how new technologies cause great companies to be overcome by smaller, more innovative ones. An example is the way small mini-mills captured market share from the giant integrated steel mills like U.S. Steel and Bethlehem Steel. Starting in the 1960s, integrated mills began developing ways to melt steel in much smaller chambers, enabling them to scale up the downstream steps in the steel-manufacturing process and shave about 20 percent off production costs.

First mini-mills targeted the least profitable portion of the steel market: rebar. Unable to compete with the low costs at which mini-mills could produce rebar, the larger integrated mills abandoned the rebar market, choosing instead to focus on higher-end market products such as angle-iron, structural beams, and sheet steel. One by one, the mini-mills penetrated each one of these higher-end markets. Each time they moved into a higher-end market, the integrated mills fled upmarket. Focused exclusively on customer demand and profit margins, the integrated mills never considered adopting the mini-mills' new, more cost-effective technology. Today, the mini-mills account for over half of the entire steel industry's production, and many of the integrated mills have gone bankrupt.

"None of the board members or executives at the integrated steel companies ever made an explicit decision to go bankrupt by handing off these markets one by one to the enemy mills," Christensen said. "But in the course of maximizing profitability and listening to the voice of the most strident customers, that's the strategy they executed on an incremental, week-by-week basis. The sum of all those incremental decisions on what they were going to prioritize caused them to flee upmarket and ultimately get killed."

Christensen sees a parallel with families that fail as a result of executing the wrong strategy. Before teaching at HBS, Christensen attended the school. At his five-year class reunion he noted that most of his classmates had secured financially lucrative employment and were happily married and raising beautiful families. Over the years, however, he observed careers and earnings that continued to climb while families and marriage relationships deteriorated. By his twenty-five-year reunion, things had changed dramatically.

"It was really quite scary to realize the proportion of our class who had gotten divorced and who were alienated or separated from their children," Christensen said. "Some of the people who were financially most successful were actually not very happy. I can guarantee that when we graduated from the Harvard Business School, not a single one of our classmates had a deliberate strategy to go out and get divorced and raise kids who were alienated. But just like the integrated steel mills, the strategy these HBS graduates implemented was to build a successful career and it was driven by this need for achievement."

The tendency to get out of balance by shifting time away from family toward business success happens gradually and often subconsciously.

"People with a high need for achievement have this unconscious drive when they have an extra half hour of time or ounce of energy to allocate that time and energy to whatever activity gives us the most important evidence that we've achieved something," Christensen said. "Of all the things that are competing for our energy and time, our careers offer by far the most tangible evidence of significant achievement. So we close a sale, ship a product, finish a project, complete a presentation, teach a great class, get paid, get promoted. All of these things are tangible evidences of our self-worth and our achievement."

Families are a different story. "Our activities with our family offer very few evidences of immediate and tangible achievements," Christensen said. "My kids misbehave every day. The house gets messy every day. So what if I'm busy tonight and don't get home until eight? My wife will still love me and my marriage will be fine because it was yesterday.

"It's not until twenty years later that you can put your hands on your hips and say I raised great kids," said Christensen. "It's a long-term investment. So people with a high need for achievement have a systematic bias to invest time and energy in those activities which, in the long run, will cause them to under-invest in relationships that will lead to the greatest health and happiness over the long run."

After graduating from HBS and before joining its faculty, Christensen worked for the Boston Consulting Group. He staked out his business and family priorities right away. Less than a month after he joined the firm, Christensen's project manager told him he had called a case meeting on the upcoming Sunday.

"I can't work on Sunday," Christensen said, explaining he had set that time apart for family and for religious worship.

His case manager became uptight and insisted that everybody in the company worked on Sundays.

Christensen apologized, but insisted he couldn't. "If that means I should not be working here, it's better to recognize that now," he told his case manager.

The manager blustered off. He returned later and said he had moved the meeting to Saturday.

"I've got a problem," Christensen told him. He explained he had made a commitment to his wife that he would not work on Saturdays either. He promised he would devote that day to his wife and their children.

This made Christensen's case manager even angrier. Christensen tried to explain that his deepest source of happiness came from intimate relationships with his children and his wife and that he would be a better and more productive employee if he had time set aside to protect those relationships.

Finally, Christensen's case manager returned a third time and said he had moved the meeting to a Friday. "Do you work on Fridays?" he asked sarcastically.

As difficult as this was for a new employee, Christensen said he was never again asked to work on Saturdays or Sundays during his tenure at Boston Consulting Group. "It just came to be known that if Christensen works for you, he doesn't do Saturdays or Sundays," he said. "If I had crossed that line just once, then I would have fought that battle every time."

To ensure he did not lose pace with his colleagues or his competitors, Christensen adopted habits at work that enabled him to increase his productivity.

First, he made sure he was the first one in the office every day, arriving routinely at 6:00 A.M. This afforded him two to three hours of uninterrupted office time per day before most colleagues got settled in.

Second, he did not leave the office for lunch or take lunch breaks. Instead, he typically brought bag lunches and ate while working at his desk. This enabled him to gain another one to two hours in lost time each day.

In the five years he was at the Boston Consulting Group, Christensen became a project manager and was instrumental in founding the firm's manufacturing strategy consulting practice. Also while at BCG he was asked to spend a year as a Fellow at the White House.

In addition to teaching at Harvard, Fortune 500 companies rely on him for expert advice. He is also a special consultant to the government in Singapore. "I'm driven to be regarded as the best in the world," Christensen said. "But then the question is: Best at what? If a person doesn't allocate time for the things that really matter, individuals find themselves having executed a strategy that produces consequences that they never intended in terms of raising a happy family."

CHAPTER 11

THE SECRET TO SUCCESS

Under any measure or standard, all the corporate leaders in this book have achieved fabulous success in their careers. This alone is not so remarkable. Plenty of individuals rise to the top of their profession. But these business leaders have reached the pinnacle of corporate America while simultaneously maintaining very rich, close family relations on top of fulfilling time-demanding service commitments to their church. That's the remarkable part—the fact that their success in the world hasn't come at the expense of their relationships at home.

So what's the secret? No doubt these guys are smart, hardworking, dedicated, and disciplined. Those qualities—along with the good fortune of timing and a few good breaks along the way—may be keys to wealth and prestigious titles. But they do not account for healthy relationships and cohesive families. Lots of bright, hard-charging professionals end up rich in the wallet and poor at home. The reason these Mormon executives have advanced so far in business while maintaining solid families is due to the women in their lives.

The wives' deep commitment to the home is also vital to the success of these CEOs' performance at work. In fact, it is inaccurate, and even misleading, to refer to the professional achievements of each of these executives without acknowledging the crucial role of his marriage partner. "All of us women have played an important role in our husbands' careers to free them up to do what they've chosen to do," said Bonnie Quigley. "I've helped Jim be who he is. There are a lot of things we [wives] take care of that they [CEOs] don't have to worry about."

The private influence these women have on their husbands is visible in these CEOs' public actions and attitudes. "I ground David," said Vicki Neeleman. "The accolades and notoriety that come with his success and his position could easily have him off on cloud nine. But around here he's just Dad. I encourage him do the kinds of things he doesn't necessarily want to do. When one of the little kids throws up on the floor, I say to David: 'Quick, get a rag.'"

The Neelemans have a saying: "Every day you should do something you don't want to do." For David, that's household chores. But on nights when David gets home in time for dinner, he often does the dishes with his daughters.

"The kids want to do dishes with their dad," Vicki said. "As soon as he's in the room, they want to do those things."

David Neeleman and these other executives know how good their wives are to them and their children, and how vital they are to the strength of their homes. These women are the glue that holds it all together: active, thriving children; busy homes; on-the-go husbands with enormous business obligations; and a time-demanding religion. As hard as these corporate leaders work to ensure the success of their companies, their wives work even harder to ensure the success of their families.

While these business leaders give up leisure and personal time to be good fathers and husbands and to serve in church capacities, their wives give up even more. These women have made a commitment to the most demanding full-time job in society: motherhood. "When you make that choice to be at home," said Cathy Crittenden, "that *is* your job. That's what you do."

Mothers know best when it comes to understanding what a stay-at-home mother does: changing diapers, packing lunches, assisting with after-school homework, driving to athletic games and dance recitals, breaking up arguments, and meting out discipline that's balanced with compassion. These tasks come without days off, pay raises, or accolades. The difficulty is magnified by the number of children at home.

"I've been willing to be at home in the trenches and do the battlefront things with the kids," said Deb Checketts, who had six children in a fourteen-year span. "As a result, Dave doesn't have to go to work worrying about whether things are being taken care of at home. This frees up a lot of his brain space to focus on what he needs to do for his company."

The personal choices each of these CEOs' wives has made are as unusual and compelling as their husbands' business successes. All but one of them were born in western Mormon communities and raised in Mormon families with heritage dating back to Mormon pioneer days. All attended college and are well educated. Some had begun careers after college. All of them chose to give up careers in favor of being stay-at-home mothers after they began having children. But their reasons and perspectives differ.

TRUE BLUE

David Neeleman and Vicki Vranes both grew up in Salt Lake City and attended rival high schools. They did not meet, however, until their families stayed in the same hotel in Arizona one winter. After returning to Utah, they dated steadily through high school graduation and up until David left for South America at age nineteen to serve his Mormon mission. While David was away, Vicki attended college and spent six months studying abroad at the Brigham Young University campus in Israel. During the entire time she wrote David every week in South America and dated no one else.

In 1980 David returned from his mission. Forty-nine days later he and Vicki married. Within a year they had their first child. During pregnancy Vicki remained in college. After the baby was born, she decided to forgo her degree and enter the workforce. David worked days and she worked nights. They maintained this arrangement until their third child was born. Around that time David got involved with his first start-up airline and Vicki quit her night job to become a full-time, stay-at-home mother.

When she was a little girl, Vicki often told her friends: "I'm going to have eight kids when I grow up." "I ended up surpassing that by one," she said. By the time David launched JetBlue in 1999, Vicki had had nine children. A seventeen-year span separates the oldest from the youngest. "I have no regrets—none," said Vicki. "I craved being a mother. I have a passion. Nothing holds a candle to motherhood and nothing is nearly as exciting to me."

Debbie and Kevin Rollins met while attending Brigham

Young University. Debbie was a sophomore and had not yet turned twenty when she decided to marry Kevin and start a family. At the time she taught dance and was taking business and general education courses. "I worked in the early years of our marriage," said Debbie. "But I knew my profession was being a mom."

For Rollins, forgoing a career for a family was not a hard choice. "I wanted a family," said Debbie. "And in order to be the best mom I could be I wanted to be with my children full time."

Debbie Rollins' mother was a working mother. "It is pretty difficult to juggle a career with being a mother," Debbie said. "My mother had the organizational and juggling skills to do that. But you are emotionally torn all the time. I applaud those women who can pull off that balancing act. Women realize that's pretty difficult to do."

Cathy Crittenden lived in Washington, D.C., and was working on the staff of Colorado senator and presidential hopeful Gary Hart when she met Gary. At the time, Gary was a student at Brigham Young University and working in Washington for Earl Butts, the secretary of agriculture. When Cathy decided to marry Gary and start a family, she eagerly left the workforce. "I never entertained the idea of going to work once we had kids," she said. "I couldn't imagine not being there and watching them grow up."

Cathy Crittenden was so insistent about being home with her children that she and Gary racked up debt to keep her home during the years Gary spent obtaining his MBA at the Harvard Business School. Gary took student loans to cover the cost of living expenses. "We did what we had to so I could be at home," Cathy said. "The alternative to loans would have been for me to go to work and put the children in day care. But we both felt strongly that once we made the decision to have children, one of us had to be home during those brief years when the kids are home."

Vicki Neeleman, Debbie Rollins, and Cathy Crittenden never really had a strong desire to work outside the home. Bonnie Quigley, on the other hand, did. She and Jim both graduated from Millard High School in 1970. Jim quarterbacked the school's football team to the Utah state championship game. Bonnie was class valedictorian. Her commencement address was titled: "Our Destiny, Our Social Responsibility."

Bonnie and Jim married after high school and both entered college. Bonnie obtained a bachelor's degree in business administration and office education. "My mother was an absolute military general in the fact that I was to have a college education and that I was not going to work simply to put Jim through school," Bonnie said. "But rather we were both going to school and expected to graduate."

Upon completing college Bonnie began a career as a schoolteacher. But after she had her second child, Bonnie decided to become a stay-at-home mother. This was no easy choice. Widowed at a young age, Bonnie's mother worked full time out of necessity. "I was raised by a working mother," Bonnie said. "I felt I'd be letting her down if I didn't continue to work."

In order to make ends meet, Jim Quigley's mother also worked during his childhood. She too was a schoolteacher. The fact that Jim grew up with a working mother had a big influence on Bonnie's decision not to be one. "As a boy Jim would come home after school and his mother wasn't home," Bonnie said. "He would go home with friends and their moms were home."

The Quigleys decided it would be to their best advantage to

have Bonnie in the home rather than in the workforce. "The major advantage is that our children would have at least one parent at home all the time," Bonnie said. "Children need stability. It's not that I was the best parent. It's for them to know that one person will always be there, whether it be Mom or Dad. Someone will always be there."

Sue Clark, wife of Harvard Business School dean Kim Clark, made the same choice Bonnie Quigley did. But the circumstances were different. Clark graduated with a degree in early childhood development. Then she entered the workforce and took a position in the Benefits Office at Harvard. She worked for Harvard for two years before having her first child. After the completion of her six-month maternity leave, Sue had a decision to make. Harvard had offered to double her salary and elevate her to a management position on the executive staff. She declined the offer and decided to remain home.

"I feel very strongly that a child needs one of its parents more than just evenings and mornings," Sue Clark said. "I just didn't want to leave my children with a baby-sitter for eight hours a day."

Kim Clark did not advise his wife to turn down Harvard's job offer; she turned it down on her own. "Part of this is cultural," she said. "We are raised this way in the Mormon faith. But I also studied this in early childhood education. Bonding for babies is critical. It was really important to me that my children bond with me when they were young."

Bonding between mothers and children is the focus of the latest wave of child-care studies. According to the Urban Institute, a Washington, D.C.–based nonprofit, half of children under age five with full-time working mothers spend at least thirty-five hours per week in child care. Yet in very young children, as little as ten hours of non-maternal child care per week can be linked to a weaker attachment or bond with the mother. The National Institute for Child Health and Human Development, which defines "child care" as "care by anyone other than the mother," suggests that the rule of thumb for maintaining a sensitive bond with a child is to keep time in child care at the lowest level that makes sense for the family.

NO COUNTRY CLUB CROWD

After earning a degree in family science, Debbie Checketts chose to be at home. "I've always resisted the temptation of joining time-consuming organizations or causes," she said. "I've always felt that in order to make the world a better place I've got to raise good children. I've got to put in the hours and the effort to do that. So rather than joining a board I've tried to be in the trenches with my kids."

The women Checketts associates with have made some different choices. "Some of my closest friends are women who have very busy and successful careers and they have great, secure, and wonderful children," said Debbie Checketts. "I admire and respect that. But for me, I had the opportunity to stay home and be in the trenches with my children and that's what I chose."

Beverly Hawes is the only woman in this book who was not raised in a Mormon home. Born in Boise, Idaho, and raised Presbyterian, Beverly had parents who each held a master's degree and worked in the field of education. Beverly's mother taught school for thirty-five years. From the time Beverly was four years old, she became accustomed to seeing her mother go off to work each day. After high school Beverly obtained a BA in education psychology from Whitman College and started teaching while working on her master's degree. Then she married Rod Hawes and chose to abandon her career plans in favor of staying home to raise children.

"It may have been helpful from a financial standpoint in the early years of our marriage if I had worked," Beverly said. "But we felt the work I would do at home was more important than the money."

Like Beverly, her husband, Rod, was not a Mormon when they married and made the decision to keep one parent home. Religion, in fact, had little to do with their decision. It stemmed from their upbringing. "Both Rodney and I came from families that were very close," Beverly said. "We knew the importance of working together for the benefit of each other and our children. We knew that family is the secret to happiness."

After Beverly had her fourth child, she and Rod joined the Mormon Church. That same year Rod got accepted to Harvard Business School. They sold their home in Boise and packed their children into a station wagon and their belongings onto a trailer for the trek to Massachusetts. Beverly had two more children and Rod went on to become one of the nation's leading mergers and acquisitions brokers in the life insurance industry. "The things that happen in the business world are very important and you can have a positive influence by working in business," Beverly said. "But the things that happen at home have eternal significance and we knew that one of us better be there to see what happens. I was fortunate to be the one. I loved it. It was the greatest experience of my life."

On one hand, the choice each of these women made to be at home with her children is made easier by the income bracket these families are in. Many mothers in much less favorable financial circumstances have no choice but to work. Wealth affords the wives of these CEOs the freedom to stay at home.

Wealth also affords resources that reduce the strains and stresses associated with child rearing. But affluence increasingly has led parents to delegate child-rearing responsibilities to child-care professionals. In declaring that "it is now possible to outsource most aspects of parenting," the *Wall Street Journal* reported in 2005 that child care is a burgeoning industry offering a wide range of services to affluent and busy families, including boutique companies that will potty-train two-year-olds, teach six-year-olds to ride a bike, and even coach parents on how to say no. According to the *Journal,* one of the leading national child-care service providers saw its placement of in-home baby nurses triple between 2000 and 2005.

Of the eight executives featured in this book, none of their wives relied on these services. They also resisted the most common form of professional child care: nannies. None of these women have ever employed a full-time or live-in nanny. For the most part, they have avoided hiring cooks and housemaids, too. "I'd be uncomfortable having any of that," said Cathy Crittenden, who raised two daughters and a son. "Homework and instrument lessons with the kids, preparing meals, chauffeuring the kids—I did all those things."

Debbie Rollins raised four children without hiring a nanny. "If you turn child rearing over to someone else, you miss out," Debbie said. "I wanted to be with my children and see them through the difficulties and the successes, rather than have them go through those experiences with someone else."

Having the resources to hire nannies and choosing not to when raising three or four children is one thing. But this practice holds even for those women raising larger families. Beverly Hawes raised six children without a nanny. "I wanted to be in the thick of it," said Beverly. "It's in the details of a child's life that a mother has her biggest impact: the meals together, the homework, passing out the breakfast cereal, hearing their little difficulties. Picking up children in the car, for example, allowed me to hear and be part of their conversations. Right after school is the most important time to be part of your children's conversations—that's when you get to the heart of what's really going on in their lives."

With nine children, Vicki Neeleman has frequently been approached by nannies desiring to work in her home. Vicki always declined. "I never went the nanny route," said Vicki. "Something always told me 'Don't go there.' I just pushed that option away. I think if I got used to having a nanny that could be my downfall; I could get comfortable being away."

In the early years of marriage, the Neelemans lived in Utah, enabling Vicki to rely on relatives to help with child care. By the time the family moved to Connecticut to start JetBlue, some of Vicki's children were teenagers. Other than help from them and an occasional baby-sitter, Vicki does the lion's share of the work at home. "Few people want to have big families or do their own housework anymore," said Vicki. "That is not posh. Nor does my work seem very important to the world. Anybody can clean, change diapers, and read to kids. Some may look at me and say that I do what others pay their nannies to do. But that's not how I look at it. I believe I have the best of everything."

Sue Clark has seven children and Deb Checketts has six. They didn't hire nannies, either. "We chose not to hire a nanny," said Sue Clark. "I wanted to be the one that taught, influenced, and directed my children's lives. The other reason I decided against nannies had to do with my early childhood studies and knowing about the way young children bond with caregivers."

This is not to say that some of these women didn't bring in outside help in some circumstances. "We had seven children in ten and a half years," said Sue Clark. "We were busy. We needed some assistance occasionally." During one of Sue's pregnancies, the Clarks hired a young woman to assist with the younger children a few hours a day.

It was common practice for most of these women to have teenage girls, often selected from their church congregation, come into the home and assist with baby-sitting and other domestic responsibilities during after-school hours and on weekend nights. For a couple years, circumstances in the Checketts' home required even more. When Deb Checketts had her sixth child, her oldest was only fourteen. With a newborn, a toddler, two elementary-school children in need of parental assistance each night with homework, a middle-school child active in sports, and a high school freshman, Deb arranged for four teenage girls from her local Mormon Church to come into her home on rotating afternoons and weeknights to help with homework and with putting the younger children to bed. At that time, Dave Checketts was CEO of Madison Square Garden and was required to attend social events in the city on most evenings. Deb tried to accompany him on an average of two nights per week, placing an even greater demand on her time at home. During this period she hired a full-time housekeeper, who resided and worked in the Checketts' home Mondays through Fridays.

"This was a practical, realistic management approach to the home," Deb Checketts said. "At that time I had a couple children who had some difficulties with some classes at school. They needed more than an hour a night with Mom. So I ran the home like a business. Practical management skills in the home are just as important as they are in a business."

With different numbers of children and with husbands whose careers put a diversity of additional demands on their time, each of these women has taken her own measures to manage her home. Their individual approaches are by no means consistent with each other. "We're not cookie-cutter women," said Deb Checketts. "We are different and have our own interests."

One way they are all alike, however, is in their attitude toward joining a country club. Just as their husbands don't golf, these women don't belong to country clubs. "The thought has never crossed my mind," said Cathy Crittenden. "I'm so uncomfortable in that situation. I don't like feeling like you have to keep up with others or portray yourself as something you are not."

Dave and Deb Checketts' property borders a prestigious country club. Yet they never joined. "We've never belonged to a country club," Deb said. "I wanted my children to have jobs in the summer and save their money for their missions. Besides, we never had time for country clubs."

IF I HAD IT MY WAY

After having nine children, Vicki Neeleman sometimes jokes with her friends: "If I had it my way, I would have a personal trainer, a perfect figure, maybe a couple of kids, and live on an island and always be in the sun." "That might actually be my view if I hadn't experienced the things I have with my family," said Vicki. "I'm living my dream now. Otherwise I wouldn't do this." "This" is working in the home full time to raise her nine children.

Hard work is not new to Vicki Neeleman. At age twelve she started working full time during the summers alongside her father. He held a management position for a large wholesaler that produced window coverings for interior decorators and department stores. Vicki would ride to work with her father and do an assortment of jobs that ranged from cleaning the factory to clerical assignments in the office. Her father often worked late. At five each afternoon Vicki would board a bus on her own and ride home. Through her teen years she earned enough money to buy her own clothes and put herself through college. When she and David first married, Vicki worked nights as a waitress while caring for her baby and two toddlers during the daytime.

Those sorts of jobs were physically exhausting. But the hardest part of motherhood is the daily grind that comes with teaching children principles, good habits, and values, such as how to work. "Trying to make children do things they don't want to do day after day is tough, very tough," Vicki said. "Nowadays, teaching children to work and clean and be respectful to each other is particularly challenging."

It entails steadily staying on top of each child and instilling in them routines. "I am the one," said Vicki, "who constantly says: 'You come in here and help clean the kitchen,' or 'Go clean the yard,' or 'Before we go out we get our work done.' I'm the drill master. I don't want to be that. But sometimes I have to be."

When David comes through the door, Vicki recruits him to help get the kids to do their chores. "I'll say to David, 'Can you take over?' And he does."

Before JetBlue, David ran Morris Air and then worked briefly as an executive for Southwest Airlines. Southwest made him sign a five-year no-compete clause, which barred him from working for a competing airline. For a while, Neeleman was home. "I loved it when he was unemployed," said Vicki. "He had to do what I do. While he loves to work, this is a different kind of work than he's used to. He was itching to get out."

Today David jokes about that experience in speeches to business groups. He seldom tells people how involved he is with his kids as a result of it. "He is so good with so many things that he does with our children," said Vicki. "He's home more than most executives, I'm sure. And he's not afraid to wash the dishes with his daughters."

Resentment can easily surface in any marriage when one spouse is gone a great deal on business and the other spouse is home grappling with the demands of child rearing. The wives of these executives are not immune from the natural frustrations that stem from this situation. "It's hard to be home with a lot of little kids," said Deb Checketts. "I was committed to stay home and *wanted* to be at home. But there were times when some resentment set in."

One of those times came when Dave Checketts was traveling on business and called home during breakfast from a hotel in Chicago. His company had reserved a suite for him on the top floor of a high-rise hotel with far-reaching views of the city's skyline. Room service had just delivered a terrific breakfast. As Dave described the view and the food to Deb, she held the phone to her ear with her shoulder while picking up Cheerios off the kitchen floor amidst the chaos of feeding her young children before school.

"It's not an easy thing," Deb Checketts said. "You have to keep constant communication going with your husband when he is traveling so resentment doesn't set in."

Cathy Crittenden first experienced this sense of frustration when Gary took his first work assignment during his days at Harvard Business School. Between work-related travel, school, and his assignments at church, he was rarely home. "I was so frustrated," she remembered. "This was my first exposure to him traveling and working around the clock."

These situations and the frustrations they generate are common. So is the tendency to complain. Crittenden chose another course, however. First, she developed interests independent of Gary's career. "That way when two people come together they have things to discuss and you're not constantly voicing your frustrations that he's never there for you."

Second, Crittenden surrounded herself with other women who provided encouragement and strength as opposed to negativity. "It is important for children to hear their mothers be supportive of their fathers and vice versa," said Crittenden. "If a mother is constantly complaining about her husband never being home and never being there for the children, she is shooting herself in the foot."

Third, Crittenden would regularly remind herself that she and Gary were a team. "We are working toward the same thing," she said. "We have to remember we are on the same team."

This approach works only if the team concept is genuine. When Cathy and Gary's children were newborn age, the two of them devised a system for handling the heavy workload at home. "When Gary would come home from the office, it was clearly fifty-fifty," Cathy said. "He gave baths, took care of babies, and changed diapers." At night, Gary made a point to get up every other night to change diapers and rock the baby back to sleep after feedings. "His willingness to do this ensured that I got one good night's sleep every other night," said Cathy. "On the nights that Gary got up with the baby, he would pay a little bit for it when he got up for work the next morning. But he was a very hands-on dad. There was no chauvinism here."

Beverly Hawes and Rod Hawes have what Beverly calls a "very well-functioning system." The system requires Rod to work very hard at his business and for Beverly to work very hard at the business of raising children who have a strong sense of self-confidence and self-worth. "The whole key is being happily married," said Beverly. "If you are happy in the partnership you can do anything and make life more productive on many fronts."

The partnership approach requires wives to be every bit as adept at time management and multi-tasking skills at home as a CEO must demonstrate in business. On the other hand, husbands must be just as willing and able to share in the duties at home. When Rod was at the busiest phase of his schooling at Harvard Business School and taking on professional assignments, Beverly became ill. For nearly a week she could scarcely get out of bed. At the time they had four little children. Rod dropped everything and devoted all his attention to the children and all domestic responsibilities for a week.

The problem was that he didn't know how to cook. He did, however, know how to grill steaks and make superb milk shakes. For five solid days he fed the children steaks and milk shakes. "Rodney, I've got to get well," Beverly told him when she discovered what he was up to. "We can't afford to eat like this."

The children loved it, however. After that experience, every time Beverly got sick the children would shout: "It's steak and milk shakes for dinner."

"Those moments are the ones where Rod's true colors shined through," said Beverly. "Even in his busiest times when he was carrying a heavy load at work, he put the children first and he made it fun for them. He did that throughout his career."

Every one of the women in this book has a very independent streak and pursues personal interests outside the home. Some of them serve on boards, some fill civic or community positions, and others are simply pursuing personal dreams and aspirations. The point is that they are not one dimensional. Their ability to perform so well as parents hinges on striking the proper balance in other areas of their life. For Vicki Neeleman that includes a vigorous personal fitness regime involving daily trips to the gym. She also manages the construction of the Neelemans' new home. Rather than hire an architect or a firm, Vicki designed the layout herself and oversees its implementation. "It's a tremendous amount of work," she said. "But I'm doing it myself, right down to mapping out the size of the vanities and mirrors to the square footage of the entryway."

A MOTHER'S INFLUENCE

The work these women do is every bit as important as the jobs their husbands have. In fact, these CEOs are the first to admit that their wives' work is even more important. But the return investment on the decision these women have made to be at home does not manifest itself in money, titles, or assets. "It is a different kind of payoff," said Bonnie Quigley. "I can't look at my 401K like Jim. I look at my children and realize that they are functioning, wonderful human beings in this world."

It's impossible to assign a dollar value to the sense of fulfillment that comes from watching a child develop. "I get tremendous joy watching my children sacrifice for each other and show love and consideration toward each other," said Vicki Neeleman. "When they are friends with each other I don't have to go out and recruit friends for them to play with. I have a great system. That's where my wealth comes from. I don't want for anything but that."

It is also difficult to attach a value to rich relationships. "My children are all grown and out of the house now," said Cathy Crittenden. "But now they are my best friends. They are the ones I talk to on the phone each day. Gary and I vacation with them. And now that they are grown up and we are having grandchildren, we'd rather be with them and they would rather be with us than anyone else."

Economic circumstances afforded all these women the option of being home. For many women today, child care is a fact of life. But more and more, high-income families are relying on the greatest amounts of child care. Meanwhile, the latest research from the National Institute of Child Health and Human Development has identified new risks with children who spend long hours in child care before age four and a half, such as poorer work habits. None of the CEOs in this book will ever be accused of having poor work habits. They are extremely driven, hard-charging individuals whose strict self-discipline has had a lot to do with their approach to business and leadership. All of these CEOs credit these qualities and habits to the influence their mothers had on them.

Kevin Rollins' mother insisted that he and his brother learn to appreciate music at a young age. When Kevin was five years old, his mother started teaching him how to play the piano and how to sing. Before long, she had Kevin performing in clubs, in front of church groups, and wherever else she could find an audience. As a child Kevin got used to performing in front of large audiences of strangers. As a CEO, Rollins is in front of large audiences of strangers all the time. "Thanks to my mother's influence, being in front of crowds and speaking in public has never scared me," said Rollins. "As a little kid, performing in front of crowds just became second nature."

Rollins developed an even more important habit under his mother's influence: practice. His mother started him on violin lessons at age five. She required him to practice for an hour a day. "When I got home from school it was hard to explain to my friends that I couldn't play football until I practiced my violin for an hour," said Rollins. "But this led to a very task-oriented, do-it-every-day mentality."

This approach is the leadership style Rollins is known for at Dell. He runs the computer company this way and expects his management team and his employees to do the same. "What I learned from my mother is that if you do things a lot and very diligently, you can get good at things," said Rollins. "The academics came naturally to me. But the hard work is something very, very different. The act of applying myself came from my mother's influence and teachings."

When Kim Clark was five years old, his mother enrolled him in an elocution program taught by a highly regarded theater coach in Salt Lake City. In the class, Clark was expected to memorize poetry, vocabulary words, scripture passages, and short dramatic sketches that he was required to present orally, while the instructor graded him on diction and voice modulation. The classes were held on Saturdays. But Mrs. Clark got up with Kim every morning at six and practiced one-on-one with him for thirty minutes. She did this with him from age five until age eleven. "She was pretty invested with me and taught me a lot," said Kim. "She had very strong views on how I should behave and what I should try to accomplish in my life."

By the time Clark was ten years old he had been in the elocution program for five years and had to complete what the school called a "capstone project." For Clark, that meant memorizing in its entirety one of the gospels of the New Testament and presenting it in a multimedia program of slides and music. Clark chose the Gospel of Luke. His mother drilled him on the memorization. Then, before his eleventh birthday, Kim stood before an audience and recited the entire Gospel of Luke, accompanied by organ music and slides of famous paintings from the life of Christ. "My mother was just intense and very high energy," said Clark. "She was always on the go. I wasn't just expected to make my bed and do dishes and chores and go to church and say prayers. She expected me to be a leader and do it well."

Clark's mother had three sayings she used to repeat to him every day as a child:

1. "Be a leader."
2. "If it's not worth doing well, it's not worth doing."
3. "Remember who you are."

On most school days, Mrs. Clark would grab Kim by the lapels of his coat before he left the house and say: "Don't you let those other kids pull you around by the nose. You be a leader. You stick to your guns. You do the right thing."

As the leader of the top business school in America, Clark embodied these simple but powerful principles taught to him by his mother beginning at age five.

Evidence of the influence these CEOs' mothers had on them and the way they conduct themselves as businessmen is easy to see. Dave Checketts' mother took the Checketts children to church every Sunday. She didn't have a driver's license. So she and the children walked, even in the winter. "Missing church was not an option," said Dave Checketts. This helps explain why Checketts developed such a rigid approach to attending church and avoiding work on Sundays.

Checketts' mother also encouraged him to seek leadership positions in school. When he ran for class president, his mother wrote his campaign speeches, calling on words from Franklin Roosevelt and John F. Kennedy. One of the speeches she wrote for her son began: "Ask not what your school can do for you, but what you can do for your school."

"In the life of a young man, a mother has a big-time influence," said Dave Checketts. "My mother was absolutely committed to honesty, hard work, and making sure that I conducted myself in a way that made her and everyone else proud. Leadership was a big deal to her. And to be a leader you must be honest, be in the right place, and be aware of how you treat others."

LIFE HAS SEASONS

Raising children and placing a heavy emphasis on family are bedrock priorities in the Mormon religion. But no matter how much marriage or children are pursued, there's no guarantee either will happen. "The statistics are pretty high for women remaining single for a long time," said Sue Clark.

These facts have led all the women interviewed for this book to encourage their daughters strongly to obtain degrees and secure the skills needed to succeed in the workforce. "I told my daughters," said Sue Clark, " 'There's one thing for sure—*you* will always be in your future. Your husband and your children, if you have that opportunity, may or may not be with you all of your life. But you will be with you all your life. So prepare yourself. There are no guarantees that you will always have someone to support you.' "

Deb Checketts gave her daughters similar advice. "There's always the chance you are not going to get married or not going to have children," she said. "I have strongly encouraged my daughters to gain an education and have a career that they can fall back on. The chances are too great that they will need to be employed at some point in their lifetime."

How have these Mormon women reacted toward daughters who have chosen careers? With full support. Gary and Cathy Crittenden's daughter Stephanie is an accountant, just like her father. She worked as an investment banker at Morgan Stanley in New York, handling mergers and acquisitions until the 9/11 terror attack. At that point, Stephanie left Manhattan and went to work for a hedge fund. Then she took a management position at Dell in its treasury department. "She's definitely her dad's daughter," said Cathy Crittenden. "We are very happy with what she's doing."

Kim and Sue Clark's oldest daughter is a full-time working mother. After earning an economics degree from the University of Utah, she accepted a professional position at the Harvard Business School. While working for HBS she also entered the school's MBA program. During this period she and her husband determined that her earning power was greater than his and that she would be the breadwinner. Her husband opted to be the stay-at-home parent.

As a result, when her second child was born, she took only a one-week leave from Harvard. Then she went immediately back to school. "The baby bonded with its father in a beautiful way," said Sue Clark. "Both parents worked well together to make it work."

Kevin and Debbie Rollins have three daughters. One is in college. The other two have degrees in business but have chosen to be stay-at-home mothers. "We put a strong emphasis on our girls completing their education," said Debbie. "Life has times and seasons. Their time right now is raising their children. But later in life they may want to work."

David and Vicki Neeleman have two daughters in college, one studying business and the other pursuing a teaching certificate for elementary education. The Neelemans' oldest daughter, Ashley, graduated from a fashion and design school in Manhattan. Married, Ashley works as an international sales representative for one of New York's leading fashion designers and has started her own business while her husband finishes his degree.

All of the women in this book had the smarts, the drive, and the talent to excel in a career and no doubt earn substantial sums of money. Each of them also had every opportunity to pursue a career, from excellent schooling and training to the right economic circumstances needed to facilitate a swift career climb. But given the choice, they all chose to invest their skills, their talents, and their resources in their children. "It saddens me to see so many young women today who feel that they have to be something other than a mother in order to be worthwhile," said Beverly Hawes. "The role of mother is downplayed and diminished in our society. Frankly, I'm grateful I know better. Motherhood is really where true joy and fulfillment is found."

When their husbands retire and look back on the product of their life's work, they will see mergers, earnings, profits, and successful businesses they helped lead.

When these mothers look back on their life's work, they will see human beings who have developed into productive, contributing members of society. And they will see future generations brought up under the same guidance. "It's very gratifying to me to see our children whenever they get together now," said Beverly Hawes. "They get along beautifully. They look out for each other and support each other. We now see it carrying over to our grandchildren. They are all turning into very happy human beings. It is a wonderful, very well-functioning system."

The system continues. The daughters of these women are following the examples of their mothers. The Hawes have three daughters. All have bachelor's degrees and two have master's degrees. Yet each has made motherhood her priority. Bonnie Quigley's only daughter, Katie, turned down a career, too. Yet she had the goods to thrive in the corporate world just like her father. "She could be the CEO of anything if she decided to," Bonnie Quigley said about her daughter, who holds two degrees and is home raising three children. "She's not intimidated by much and she can keep a lot of balls in the air at the same time. She is certainly as capable as any man on the block."

The biggest influence the Mormon religion has on these women's choices may be the emphasis the Church's teachings place on making decisions based on a long-term perspective. All of these Mormon women who are married to the CEOs in this book view their decision to be at home as a seasonal one. "There are seasons in life," said Sue Clark. "Once childbearing years are over there are many years to pursue education and other things. But there are seasons and it's essential to protect and guard these childbearing years because they are shorter than life expectancy. There is a narrow window for childbearing and child rearing."

Vicki Neeleman has watched her husband build an airline from the ground up. She has her own dream to design something: homes and neighborhoods. She already has an architectural scheme in mind, right down to the cobblestone walkways and old-fashioned, gas-burning streetlamps. "I'm at home now," she said. "But as soon as this is over, I want to fly, too. When the season is right, I will."

CHAPTER 12

SUDDENLY OUT OF NOWHERE

"An organization and its leader are judged on how they act and be-have in tough times."

—Ken Chenault, CEO at American Express

September 11, 2001
American Express Corporate Headquarters
#1 World Financial Center
51st Floor

The view from Gary Crittenden's conference room on the top floor of World Financial Center #1 was one of the most far-reaching in Lower Manhattan. He could see across the Hudson River to Jersey City, down the Hudson to the Statue of Liberty, and across West Street to the North Tower of the World Trade Center. Crittenden was chairing a meeting against the backdrop of this view when an approaching aircraft drowned out his voice. Everyone stopped talking.

Military jets occasionally fly up the Hudson, but Crittenden knew instantly this was no military exercise. The engine noise was too close, too loud, too fast. He turned to the window and saw American Airlines Flight 11, a Boeing 767 carrying passengers and 10,000 gallons of fuel, approaching at 470 miles per hour. Silent, Crittenden watched the jet bypass his building and plow into the North Tower of the World Trade Center across the street, producing a giant ball of fire.

Crittenden stared out the window until smoke began to pour from the top floors of the North Tower. He and his colleagues immediately turned on CNN. American Express CEO Ken Chenault was in Salt Lake City working out of the company's operating center. Many other executives were traveling on business. Crittenden was one of two senior corporate officers in the building. He picked up his phone and dialed his wife, Cathy, at home.

"A terrible disaster has occurred," he told her. "A plane hit one of the Twin Towers."

"What are you talking about?" Cathy said. "It hasn't been on TV."

"It will be," he said before assuring her that he was okay.

She asked what he was going to do.

Wait, he said, to see what happens next.

JIM, WE NEED YOU NOW

#2 WORLD FINANCIAL CENTER
DELOITTE & TOUCHE CORPORATE HEADQUARTERS
8:47 A.M.

Forty-nine-year-old Jim Quigley did not see or hear the plane strike the North Tower. He was speaking to thirty employees in

Deloitte's third-floor conference room overlooking the Hudson River when an assistant opened the door. "Jim, we need you. And we need you now!"

Quigley excused himself, ducked out, and hurried up to his ninth-floor office. A group of senior Deloitte partners were waiting for him. One of them pointed at the television monitor. Quigley watched the news in silent disbelief.

"What are we going to do?" one partner asked.

Quigley had 3,500 employees in the World Financial Center office, which is adjacent to the American Express office tower and directly across the street from the Trade Center. He and his partners contemplated evacuating. Then a broadcast message from the building security indicated that the incident at the North Tower did not impact their building and everyone should stay put.

Quigley and his co-regional managing partner, Bill Freda, sent word to their leadership partners to assemble at once to discuss a possible evacuation order in the event that conditions changed.

WHERE ARE OUR PLANES?

JetBlue Headquarters
Queens, New York

The future could not have been brighter for David Neeleman. After launching JetBlue two years earlier as an upstart private company, he was ready to take the airline public. Shortly after 9:00 A.M. on Wall Street, investment bank Morgan Stanley planned to hold JetBlue's IPO, hoping to raise $150 million in capital from new investors in the airline.

Back in Connecticut, David had another deal about to close. Since moving to Connecticut from Utah, the Neelemans had wanted to build a home. After an exhaustive search for land, David and Vicki had finally found the ideal spot not far from their existing home in New Canaan. Shortly after JetBlue's IPO got underway, David and Vicki were scheduled to sign closing documents and purchase the land.

The decision to hold JetBlue's IPO on September 11 hinged on the airline's rapid growth. In 1999, JetBlue started with $130 million. It began operating out of New York's John F. Kennedy International Airport in February 2000, and by August 2001 it had expanded into sixteen markets with seventy-nine flights daily. Just two weeks prior to September 11 JetBlue had opened a West Coast base of operations out of Long Beach, California. All of this had reduced JetBlue's cash balance to $42 million. Meanwhile, to keep up with his company's rapid growth, Neeleman had ordered approximately 100 new jets from Airbus, creating an even greater need for more cash.

JetBlue's legal counsel, Tom Kelly, and chief financial officer, John Owen, were in the Wall Street area preparing final copies of the prospectus for the IPO. Expecting a call from them any minute, Neeleman and JetBlue's management team gathered around a conference room table at corporate headquarters. They were less than thirty minutes away from a $150 million payday that would further propel them past their competitors.

Suddenly an employee poked his head into the conference room. "A plane just hit the World Trade Center," he said.

Neeleman and his colleagues assumed that a small plane had

probably gone astray and accidentally hit the tower. They flipped on the television. It showed the tail of a commercial jet sticking out of the North Tower. "This is not just some little plane that got led astray," Neeleman said.

A few minutes later, Neeleman watched on television as a second plane approached Lower Manhattan and struck the South Tower. It confirmed Neeleman's fear: A terrorist attack was under way. And the terrorists were using passenger jets as weapons. Neeleman could tell from the television that the second plane was not operated by JetBlue. But what if more planes had been hijacked? New York City is JetBlue's hub.

"Where are our planes?" Neeleman wanted to know at once.

Neeleman and his team immediately activated the company's emergency command center at corporate headquarters and set out to make contact with every JetBlue pilot and get immediate answers to two questions:

"Are our crew members safe?"

"Are our customers safe?"

HOW MANY PEOPLE DO WE HAVE IN THE TOWER TODAY?

Jim Quigley, Bill Freda, and Deloitte's leadership team had assembled in Quigley's office and had barely begun discussing ways to evacuate in an orderly manner when the room shook and the air echoed like a thunderclap. To Quigley, it felt like an earthquake. Stunned, he spun toward the television monitor just in time to see a ring of fire sweep around the South Tower. Now he had no doubt a terrorist attack was under way. "We're evacuating," Quigley said. "Get everybody out of this building."

With both Trade Center towers hit by planes within a fifteen-minute span, some Deloitte partners feared their building might be next. Quigley and his senior partners split up, each one taking responsibility for one of the firm's nine floors. They personally walked the floors, inspecting every office, every cubicle, and every bathroom to ensure that every employee was out and that none were left behind due to injury. While canvassing his floor, Quigley placed a cell phone call to Bonnie at home, assuring her that he was okay.

Bonnie had been watching television and asked him what he was going to do next. He didn't know, he told her before hanging up.

Quigley and Freda were responsible for all Deloitte Tri-State employees, including 3,500 employees working at the firm's World Financial headquarters. Accounting for them posed a challenge. Forced into unfamiliar emergency exit stairwells, some employees got disoriented and accidentally emerged on West Street, directly across the street from the World Trade Center. "For some of my people it was just tragic what they saw," said Quigley. "If you believe in the sanctity and dignity of human life, they saw things that you just shouldn't see."

Most exited onto the plaza between World Financial Tower and the Hudson River. Quigley and his administrative assistant, Ava Sloane, huddled with ten senior Deloitte associates in the courtyard of the plaza. "How many people do we have in the Tower today?" Quigley shouted amidst the chaos.

Some of Deloitte's biggest clients, such as Merrill Lynch and Marsh & McClelland, had offices in the Trade Center. On any given day, hundreds of Deloitte professionals worked in those offices. Normally, a few clicks on a Deloitte computer would pull up the precise whereabouts of every Deloitte employee working in the North and South Towers. But all laptops and most cell phones had been left behind in the rush to get out of the building. Quigley and his colleagues lacked the traditional communication links that Deloitte relied on to run its operation.

A full accounting of employees would require a manual head count. But approximately 50,000 people from the Financial District had spilled into the plaza space. Deloitte employees were intermingled with all the others.

An accountant his entire career, Quigley had been trained to solve large-scale financial disasters that occur on paper. Now he had to account for employees caught in a tragedy. No Deloitte handbook offered instructions. He and his partners improvised. They devised a two-pronged strategy: First, locate and round up as many Deloitte schedulers as possible and have them identify employees working in the World Trade Center. Second, record a message with reporting instructions on the company's emergency 800 number. Every Deloitte employee at the World Financial office had an 800 number on his or her ID badge and knew to call it for instructions in times of emergency.

Suddenly Ava Sloane screamed. People had begun jumping from the top floors of the World Trade Center. Quigley grabbed Sloane by her shoulders and spun her toward the Hudson River. "Ava, don't look at that building!" Quigley said sternly. "Don't look at that building anymore. Look out at the river."

People continued to jump. And the scene in the plaza worsened. Some of Quigley's partners felt edgy. They feared they were sitting ducks for another terrorist strike.

They divided up. One group of partners took the schedulers and headed to the ferries in hopes of crossing the river to the company's Jersey City office. It still had phones, computers, and its e-mail system. Quigley led a smaller group of partners and administrative assistants two blocks south of the World Trade Center to the Battery Park City apartment of senior Deloitte partner Henry Ferraro. There Quigley hoped to quickly record a message on the company's employee hot line. If separated, all parties agreed to meet up at the company's Jersey City office.

At Ferraro's building, six members of Quigley's party remained in the concierge area on the ground floor. Ferraro's apartment is on the twenty-fourth floor. The group feared using elevators in a high-rise just two blocks from the Trade Center. Quigley and one other partner agreed to go up.

Once inside, Quigley used the phone first to track down Deloitte's senior security administrator to obtain instructions on how to access and record a message on the company's emergency 800 number. He had never had to do it previously. After recording the message instructing employees on how to report their whereabouts, Quigley began placing calls to Deloitte schedulers in hopes of determining which employees were inside the Trade Center.

DROP EVERYTHING

Vicki Neeleman had not been around a television or a radio all morning. She couldn't understand why David hadn't called her about the real estate closing. They were late. She called his cell phone.

"We've got to sign these papers," she told him. "We've got to get the check there."

"Vicki, do you know what's happening?" he said.

"No. What is it?"

Hurriedly, he explained two planes had been hijacked and flown into the World Trade Center. He worried a JetBlue plane could be next.

"Drop everything," he said before hanging up. "We're not buying any land."

RUN FOR YOUR LIFE

It took Gary Crittenden and 3,000 American Express employees about thirty minutes to evacuate their offices. Once assured that all the people were out, Crittenden and four other American Express officials tried to establish a command post at the firm's security desk in the main lobby of the building, but NYPD quickly took over that space. Crittenden and his colleagues needed a communication center to verify the safety and whereabouts of their company's employees. Like Deloitte, American Express had employees who worked with clients in the Trade Towers.

With everyone running out of the building and EMTs and police officers milling around the lobby, Crittenden took four colleagues and headed in the opposite direction, back up forty-eight floors to the firm's public affairs office near the top of the building.

The building was empty. But all communication links were still operative: computers, the Internet, and phones. Crittenden and his colleagues initiated an effort to track every American Express employee working in World Financial Center and the World Trade Center, as well as all those traveling to New York. While working the phones, Crittenden kept his eye on CNN to monitor events unfolding across the street.

At ten o'clock, the American Express building suddenly started rocking. The television went dead. So did all computers, phones, and lights. Crittenden did not know that the South Tower had just collapsed. He and his colleagues figured their building had been hit by a plane. They were near the top floor of an evacuated building. Virtually no one knew they were up there. The only way out was down forty-seven flights of stairs. Terrified, Crittenden and his colleagues headed for the emergency stairwell.

Crittenden is a long-distance runner in excellent physical shape. But no regimen had conditioned him to run down forty-seven flights of stairs amidst a terrorist strike. At the nineteenth floor he smelled smoke. Fearful that the floors beneath him were burning, he kept running.

Fifteen minutes later Crittenden and his team reached the ground floor. They opened the emergency stairwell door leading into the main lobby. It was filled with smoke. They retreated back into the stairwell and slammed the door shut, and ran toward a rear stairwell exit that led to the American Express parking garage.

Moments later Crittenden emerged onto the street. The first man he encountered was bleeding profusely from a gash running from his forehead down his face.

"What happened? What happened?" Crittenden asked.

The man had been hit by falling glass. He told Crittenden that bombs planted in the first floor of the South Tower had exploded.

Fearing that bombs might be in other surrounding buildings, Crittenden worked his way toward the Hudson River in hopes of catching a boat to Jersey City, where American Express maintained a satellite office. He couldn't call his wife to assure her that he was out of the building; he had left his cell phone behind in his rush to evacuate.

ALL ALONE

Jim Quigley was still in his partner's twenty-fourth-story apartment two blocks from the World Trade Center when the South Tower collapsed. He ran to the window in time to see throngs of people running away from the Trade Center, trailed by a rushing wall of ash and smoke. Police, fire, and rescue personnel were running in the opposite direction, toward the Trade Center. Within minutes Quigley could not see across the street; the ash in the air was too thick.

As soon as the dust settled, Quigley rushed down twenty-four flights of stairs to the street in search of his six colleagues who had been waiting for him. They were gone. The streets were abandoned. A stranger emerged through the ash. "Put this on," the man said, handing Quigley a mask.

Quigley applied it to his face and went searching for Ava, Bill Freda, and his partners. Knowing they would not run toward the towers, Quigley headed south toward the lower tip of Manhattan. Then he worked his way west toward the Hudson. His assistant and his partners were nowhere in sight. Neither was anyone else.

All alone on an ash-covered street, Quigley turned back toward his partner's Battery Park apartment. He didn't know where any of his people were, and no one knew his whereabouts.

LOSING $150 MILLION IN A DAY

It took just minutes for JetBlue officials to activate the emergency command center at corporate headquarters. David Neeleman stared at the monitor for the systems computer that tracks all Jet-

Blue airplanes that are in flight. It showed five blue planes in the air. A host of others were taxiing for takeoff at various airports along the Eastern Seaboard. Communications with pilots on each plane confirmed that none had been penetrated by hijackers.

Shortly after JetBlue's planes were confirmed safe, the FAA ordered all commercial flights in the United States grounded. All airborne flights had to land at once. Within minutes, pilots on JetBlue's five airborne flights received orders to touch down in Wichita, Raleigh-Durham, Kansas City, and other venues.

This posed a challenge. JetBlue flies direct between the East and West Coasts and between New York and Florida. It does not fly in or out of any of these Midwestern and southern airports. As a result, it had no crew members and no airport personnel on the ground to receive these flights in places like Wichita and Raleigh-Durham. Nor did its passengers live in those cities. All of them would need ground transportation, lodging, and food.

At corporate headquarters, JetBlue employees were divided into teams. Each team took responsibility for a flight. As the flights touched down, teams began finding hotel space, lining up ground transportation from the airport, and arranging for meals.

In the midst of all this, Neeleman got a call from the lead banker at Morgan Stanley who was handling the IPO. The news was grim. By this time a third plane had struck the Pentagon and a fourth plane had been downed in Pennsylvania. With all domestic air travel grounded indefinitely, the future of the airline industry was in turmoil, surrounded by uncertainty. There was no way investors would step forward now to invest in JetBlue. Morgan Stanley had called off JetBlue's IPO indefinitely.

Neeleman's cell phone rang again. It was his CFO calling from the Wall Street area. He had talked to the Securities and Exchange

Commission and received confirmation that they could still go through with the IPO.

Forget it, Neeleman told him, urging him to flee the area as soon as possible.

In a matter of hours, $150 million had vanished. Yet Neeleman and his airline were still on the hook for an entire new fleet of jets from Airbus. Without the IPO he didn't know how he would pay for them. Worse still, Neeleman had over 4,000 employees whose job security was now in question.

Neeleman ducked out of the command center and went up to a conference room. Alone, he stared out the window toward the World Trade Center towers, one collapsed and one burning. Numb and silent, he watched and wondered: Who is going to want to fly again?

CHAPTER 13

PUT YOUR SHOULDER TO THE WHEEL

Unable to find his colleagues, Jim Quigley returned to his partner's twenty-fourth-story apartment in Battery Park. He hiked back up twenty-three flights of stairs and recorded an updated message on Deloitte's employee hot line. Next he established phone contact with the Jersey City office. Then he resumed calling schedulers in an attempt to verify how many Deloitte employees were in the World Trade Center.

Just when he thought things couldn't get worse, they did. Just after ten-thirty, the North Tower of the World Trade Center collapsed. Deloitte's phone switch for the firm's Tri-State offices in New York City, Jersey City, Long Island, and Stamford, Connecticut, was housed in the North Tower. When the second tower fell, Deloitte lost its Tri-State phone network and voice-mail system.

Instantly, everyone in Quigley's partner's apartment building was ordered to evacuate. Quigley made another trek down twenty-three flights of stairs and with his partner headed toward the Hudson River in hopes of reaching Jersey City by ferry.

The collapse of the Trade Center towers touched off a barrage of phone calls into the Quigley residence in New Canaan. In emergency and disaster situations, a bishop in the Mormon Church has to account for every church member and assess their needs. In 2001 Quigley had close to 500 members in his New Canaan congregation.

The Church has a tiered system in place to expedite this process: At all times a certain percentage of men and women in each Mormon congregation are assigned three to five homes or families to look after in times of trouble. So, for example, in a flood, a woman who has five families on her contact list would telephone or otherwise communicate with those families and then report that information to the bishop. This enables a bishop to quickly develop a head count and assess the needs of his congregation without personally locating every member.

Bonnie Quigley knew Jim could not oversee his duties as bishop. His first priority would be his people at Deloitte; the Church would want it no other way.

Bonnie's only question was how far Jim would go to fulfill his obligations to his company. "My mind was racing," she recalled. "Jim had a lot of people working in the two Trade Towers. I was wondering, Would Jim actually go over there and try to do a head count?"

Unable to get through to Jim's cell phone, Bonnie focused on fielding calls from Mormons in New Canaan who were eager to help account for members of their congregation. A friend from church volunteered to track down and account for the whereabouts of every New Canaan Mormon working in New York City on 9/11: twelve in all, including Quigley, Neeleman, and Critten-den. Working the phones, it became clear that those closest to the World Trade Center would be the hardest to reach.

Cathy Crittenden had not heard from Gary since the towers had collapsed. Cathy's calls to Gary's cell phone had gone unanswered. He had left it behind when he fled his building.

Cathy had heard from her daughter Stephanie, an investment banker at Morgan Stanley. She and her roommate, a young, female college student from Utah, had escaped Lower Manhattan and fled by ferry to New Jersey, where they were stranded.

Unable to locate Jim, Bonnie fielded a call from her twenty-year-old son, Morgan, who was serving a full-time, two-year French-speaking mission for the Church in New York City. Normally, Mormon missionaries are not permitted to telephone home except on Mother's Day and special holidays such as Christmas. But the Church's mission president in Scarsdale knew that Morgan's father worked across the street from the Trade Center and told him to call home to check on his father. When Morgan's mission president learned that Bonnie had not heard from her husband, he invited Bonnie to come to the mission office in Scarsdale to spend the afternoon with her son. Morgan, at the time, was fielding calls from hundreds of Mormon parents around the United States who were concerned about the safety and whereabouts of their sons and daughters assigned to New York City. Bonnie left her house and arrived in Scarsdale within an hour.

The North Tower was still standing when Gary Crittenden made it across the Hudson to American Express's satellite office in Jersey City. He discovered a makeshift morgue on the side lawn, where rescue workers were processing deceased persons who had been ferried across from Manhattan. With most of the company's senior executives traveling, Crittenden was the only member of the company's management team who could actually see the tower. He remained on the phone with senior members of the company, giving periodic updates concerning the condition of American Express's building. While watching the windows, Crittenden saw the North Tower collapse and hit the American Express building starting at the twenty-sixth floor. It would be six months before he would be back in the office.

Once the second tower collapsed, his focus shifted to 7 World Trade Center, a much smaller building in the World Trade Center complex. It housed much of American Express's backup communications capability. With that building facing collapse, Crittenden and a few critical employees in Jersey City initiated efforts to transfer those communications systems to another facility.

In the midst of this effort, Crittenden used a borrowed cell phone to call Cathy at home to assure her that he was safe. He asked the whereabouts of their daughter Stephanie and her roommate. Cathy informed him they were somewhere in New Jersey. Gary instructed Cathy to get ahold of his driver. "Tell him to find the girls in New Jersey and get them home," he said. "I'll make my way home."

Quigley's journey to Jersey City took longer. After his boat was detoured to Liberty Island, he walked a mile along the river until he reached a light rail system that delivered him to Jersey City. He walked a few more blocks to Deloitte's Jersey City office. There Quigley found his administrative assistant, Ava Sloane, and the rest of the group he had last seen on the street below his partner's twenty-fourth-story Battery Park apartment.

Deloitte's Jersey City office lost its phone service when the North Tower collapsed. But computers and printers still worked. The head of Deloitte's human resource department printed personnel lists of all 3,500 employees, broken down by areas of responsibility. With the lists in hand, Quigley, Freda, and over twenty Deloitte partners filed into cars at the Jersey City office and headed toward the firm's Parsippany, New Jersey, office, which still had phone service and e-mail access.

As the day wore on, David Neeleman telephoned Vicky from his JetBlue office, assuring her that he was safe, and informed her that he would be home very late. He'd be bringing JetBlue's legal counsel, Tom Kelly, with him. Kelly lives in Salt Lake City and had flown into New York for the IPO. Without a way home, he needed a place to stay. Vicki passed on the news that some of their neighbors had already lost loved ones, and that fellow church member Jim Quigley and Gary Crittenden still had not been accounted for. "I recognized that my sons had a few friends whose fathers weren't going to be coming home," Neeleman recalled. "And I knew that Jim and Gary were right across the street and I knew the trouble they were going through."

With everything seemingly collapsing around him, Neeleman returned to the command center. "I had to stay focused," Neeleman said. "No one wants to see their leader coming apart at the seams."

He focused his employees' attention on the fact that all their planes had landed safely, all crew members were unharmed, and all JetBlue customers were on the ground and being taken care of with lodging accommodations. Then Neeleman retreated to his office.

"My primary job is to look to the future," Neeleman said. "Are we going to have money next week? Are we going to have the ability to restart the airline?"

On a piece of paper he jotted down reasons why people wouldn't want to fly:

1. Fear.
2. The hassle associated with increased airport security.
3. Mourning. Much of JetBlue's customer base is New Yorkers flying south to Florida to vacation. Nobody would feel like having fun at Walt Disney World when thousands of New Yorkers had lost their lives.
4. Economic uncertainty. Terrorism causes job loss and makes people less likely to spend money on leisure travel.

The one that concerned him most was fear. What would it take to overcome people's fear about flying?

By 2:00 P.M. every New Canaan Mormon working in New York City had been accounted for except for Jim Quigley. Bonnie still had not heard from him, and calls to his cell phone were not going through.

It was nearly 4:00 P.M. when Bonnie's son Morgan drove her back home from the mission office in Scarsdale. As she said goodbye to her son, her cell phone rang. It was Jim. He was in Parsippany and had no idea how late in the day it was or that seven hours had passed since he'd last spoken to Bonnie. "I was so focused on finding my people that I lost track of time," Quigley said.

The call ended quickly with Jim saying he would be home late. Then he and Bill Freda gathered their partners in the Parsippany office and issued assignments. Each partner received an employee list and was given responsibility to account for every employee on his list.

The 7 World Trade Center building that housed American Express's backup communications systems collapsed while Crittenden was in the company's Jersey City office. But American Express successfully transferred those systems to another facility. After that transfer was complete and Crittenden had made telephone contact with the rating agencies and corporate executives around the United States, there was nothing more he could do in Jersey City but try to find his way home.

He took a bus to the Penn Station terminal in Newark in hopes of getting a train that would take him toward Connecticut. But train service was down. Crittenden walked the streets in search of a taxi but couldn't find one. Then he spotted an African-American man standing near a beat-up pickup truck. Crittenden offered to pay him for a ride home.

The stranger agreed to do it for $800.

Crittenden negotiated the price down to $600 and hopped in.

As the driver navigated through the streets of Newark, Crittenden felt uneasy. He asked the driver what he did for work. The driver said he had just gotten out of prison.

When the driver inexplicably passed by the entrance ramp to the New Jersey Turnpike and instead pulled into an alley crowded with men standing around a car, Crittenden got a bad feeling. He ran through his mind all the things he had already experienced during the day and feared the worst was ahead.

The driver got out, saying he wanted to ask his friends if he could borrow their car for the long drive to New Canaan. Afraid he would be beaten up or robbed, Crittenden waited nervously in the truck. Moments later the driver returned and said his friends wouldn't let him borrow the car. He backed out of the alley and headed toward the turnpike.

Nearly two hours later the stranger pulled into Crittenden's circular driveway in New Canaan. Crittenden paid him $600 in cash and the man drove off, never to be heard from again.

Thirty minutes later Gary's personal driver pulled into the driveway and Gary's daughter Stephanie and her roommate emerged from the car. "It was a miracle Gary's driver found them," said Cathy. "The girls didn't even know where they were in New Jersey."

Jim Quigley lives minutes from Crittenden. But he was hours from being ready to head home. He determined to stay in Parsippany until he got reports from every partner responsible for finding employees. The partner in charge of Deloitte's mergers and acquisitions unit was the first to report back. All 160 members in that unit were equipped with BlackBerries, and within two hours of being contacted every person reported back, confirming his or her safety and whereabouts. The other partners had to rely on phones and e-mails.

By the end of the night, all but ten of Deloitte's 3,500 World Financial Center employees had been accounted for. Quigley was in his car headed home around 11:30 P.M. when one of his partners called him from the Jersey Turnpike. In tears and pulled over on the shoulder, the partner reported that he had just heard from the last of the missing employees on his list. Everyone on his list was now accounted for and safe.

It was nearly midnight when Quigley's driver finally delivered him to his home. Bonnie waited for him at the door as he approached, haggard and speckled in ash. Once inside the house, they knelt and cried and prayed. They had a lot to be thankful for.

Eight years earlier Deloitte occupied the top floors of office space in the North Tower. After terrorists bombed the building in 1993, Deloitte decided to vacate and move across the street to World Financial Center. Cantor Fitzgerald took over the Deloitte office space in the North Tower. None of the Cantor Fitzgerald employees inside the tower on 9/11 survived. Had Deloitte not moved in 1993, Jim would have been on one of the top five floors of the Trade Center when the plane struck, along with 2,000 Deloitte employees. None of them would have survived.

When they finished praying, the Quigleys climbed into bed. Within minutes Jim was asleep.

David Neeleman was the last of the three men to reach home. He and his corporate attorney left JetBlue's headquarters well after midnight. As David drove over the Whitestone Bridge, it was deserted. None of the toll booths were manned and the toll gates were stuck in the open position. Nothing was normal.

Neeleman couldn't stop thinking about cockpits and pilots. Each of the planes that hit the Trade Center towers and the Pentagon were taken over by terrorists who had penetrated the cockpit. Cockpit doors are designed for egress, enabling pilots to get out quickly in case of emergency. But this also enables hijackers to penetrate the cockpit at will.

"Who is going to want to get on an airplane when you have the ability to just kick down the cockpit door?" he asked himself.

By the time he got home it was after 2:00 A.M. Vicki had fallen asleep waiting for him. She awoke while David and Tom Kelly warmed up a can of soup. She found them in the kitchen. David was quiet and looked sad and depressed, emotions totally out of character for her husband. "Something happened to him," Vicki said. "A chunk of his heart got bitten off."

He went to bed exhausted but had trouble sleeping. He had formulated in his mind a plan to reinforce cockpits. He wanted bulletproof cockpit doors installed in every JetBlue airplane. The sooner he could get back to the office and get going on refitting airplanes for higher safety standards, the better.

CHAPTER 14

SIMPLE BOYS

In 1968, Jim Quigley masterfully quarterbacked the Eagles from small, rural Millard High School to the Utah State Championship football game, played at BYU's Cougar Stadium in Provo. There Jim experienced something he wasn't used to: defeat. In losing to Delta High School, Jim had thrown three interceptions and fumbled once. After the game, Jim sat at his locker, tears streaming down his face.

The father of one of Jim's teammates approached him in an effort to lend support. "I respect you and your abilities, and I appreciate your leadership and your mind," the boy's father told Jim. "You will be back. Hold your head up."

By the time the team had boarded the bus for the long journey home, Jim still had not removed his football uniform. Jim's father told the coach not to wait. Mr. Quigley said he and his wife would drive their son home. After thirty minutes alone in the shower, Jim's tears finally stopped. Then he dressed and filed into the backseat of his parents' car.

Few words were spoken during the drive home. But Jim's mother took advantage of the opportunity to teach her son a valuable lesson that stayed with him throughout his business career. "My mother encouraged me," Jim recalled. "My lesson was that sports can provide a window into life, and teach that sometimes it does not go your way. You must pick yourself up and go forward. The sun does rise again."

That attitude—learned by a boy on a ball field in Utah—took hold when Jim Quigley got out of bed at 5:30 in the morning on September 12, 2001. Quigley's personal calendar indicated he had a major reception to attend that day for new Deloitte partners at Windows on the World, the restaurant occupying the 110th floor of the World Trade Center, but the famous restaurant no longer existed. His tightly programmed schedule no longer mattered. His company and all of America had been dealt a bitter defeat by terrorists.

Quigley dressed and left home shortly after 6:00 A.M. and headed for Parsippany. This time there was no time for tears. By noon the last ten Deloitte employees were accounted for. Only one, a man who was in the Marsh & McClelland offices in the North Tower at the time of the crash, did not survive.

With his people accounted for, Quigley's attention immediately shifted to rebuilding the firm's vast communications network and reestablishing the company's infrastructure. Deloitte performs accounting and auditing for 25 percent of the Fortune 1000 companies in the United States. And it provides tax advice and financial service consulting to nearly a third of the companies in the Fortune 1000. Its clients include General Motors, Procter & Gamble, Merrill Lynch, MCI, and many others. To service these companies, Deloitte relies on a cutting-edge technology that enables partners to be mobile.

"The mobile model is so dependent on cell phones, laptops, e-mail, computers, and office systems," Quigley said. "When you take those things away you discover how dependent you are on technology."

Restoring these tools was complicated by the fact that Deloitte's financial headquarters was indefinitely off limits, the firm's phone switch was destroyed, and many of its computers and systems were damaged in the attack. If they didn't figure out a way to recover quickly, clients from the auto industry to pharmaceuticals to financial services across the country would be impacted.

BE DECISIVE

On the ride into work on September 12, David Neeleman had one thing on his mind: saving his airline. Less than twenty-four hours after the first plane struck the World Trade Center, Neeleman telephoned Airbus and told them he wanted bulletproof cockpit doors installed in every JetBlue airplane.

Airbus indicated it didn't have a door design like the one Neeleman envisioned. But Airbus suggested Swiss Air might. Neeleman called Swiss Air next and told them what he wanted. He pushed for design drawings on his desk before the end of the day. Later that day the plans arrived via fax at JetBlue's headquarters in Queens.

The plans were taken to JetBlue's maintenance team with instructions to figure out how to refit the existing planes with bulletproof cockpit doors. JetBlue's legal team got to work on obtaining approval from the FAA to install them.

Reinforcing doors wasn't all Neeleman had in mind. He

wanted every JetBlue airplane outfitted with four cabin security cameras with a live video feed to the cockpit, enabling pilots to see what is transpiring in the cabin. No airline had this feature and no airplane manufacturer had plans in existence for this. So Neeleman instructed his own design unit to get busy developing this capability for JetBlue planes.

DELEGATE

Surrounded by his firm's top partners, Quigley assured them that together they could restore the company to full working capacity fast enough to enable their clients not to suffer poor service. Everyone bought into his can-do attitude. And everyone agreed to do whatever it took to get it done.

The firm's chief information officer was in Los Angeles. Unable to fly, he rented a car, bought two cell phones, and immediately began driving back to New York to help recover the firm's infrastructure. While driving across country he contacted via cell phone every hardware vendor that does business with Deloitte and made arrangements for additional servers to be brought into the firm's New Jersey offices.

Meanwhile, Quigley delegated the tasks to recover the mobile communications model rapidly. He put a partner in charge of cell phones, a partner in charge of laptops, a partner in charge of finding alternative office space, and a partner in charge of client communications. The partners than went and got what Deloitte needed.

AT&T Wireless provided Deloitte with 1,000 cell phones.

Toshiba, IBM, and Hewlett-Packard provided 1,000 new laptops.

And Marriott Hotels agreed to vacate five entire floors at its Midtown Marriott Marquis and rent them to Deloitte for temporary office space.

All of this was achieved by the end of the day on September 12.

Quigley then dispatched a team of twenty-five people equipped with bolt cutters and suitcases to the firm's downtown office to recover thousands of laptops. The entire area beneath Fourteenth Street had been shut down by New York City authorities. But Deloitte got special permission from the city to drive cargo vans as far as the makeshift barricades erected on Fourteenth Street, and then walk from there to the Deloitte offices across the street from Ground Zero. Once inside their offices, Quigley's men used bolt cutters to cut the cables securing the laptops to desks. The computers were then stacked in suitcases, which were carried down eight and nine flights of stairs to the street. The team wheeled the suitcases up to Fourteenth Street and loaded them into the cargo vans, which were driven to the Marriot Marquis. There, all the beds and hotel furniture on five floors had been removed and replaced by folding tables. The laptops were spread out on the tables and technicians cleaned them, removing all dust, ash, and asbestos.

Quigley sent out an e-mail to all company employees informing them they could pick up their laptops at the Marriott. Those whose laptops were destroyed were told to report to the Parsippany office to pick up brand-new ones. All employees who lost cell phones in the disaster were also told to report to Parsippany to pick up new phones.

Within one week all 3,500 displaced Deloitte employees were reequipped with laptops and cell phones, enabling them to work from remote locations. While this was going on, Deloitte's technology team went in and wired all five floors of the Marriott space for phones and Internet, creating an instant communications infrastructure. Within one week Deloitte's entire tax department was relocated to the Marriott, which had been converted into a fully operational office space.

An additional 1,000 downtown Deloitte employees were moved into the firm's Midtown office, doubling that office's capacity. Leading by example, Quigley moved into that building and shared an office with Bill Freda to conserve space.

Another 1,000 downtown employees were relocated to the Parsippany office, doubling its occupancy. The firm's Jericho, Long Island, office took on 150 new employees and the Stamford, Connecticut, office added a bunch of employees from downtown. The last 100 displaced Deloitte employees were put in spare office space offered up by a law firm that does business with Deloitte.

In a little over a week, all 3,500 Deloitte employees were established in a half-dozen temporary offices around the Tri-State area, all fully equipped with the communication tools they needed to perform their jobs. They operated that way for a year.

"When you have an organization that you depend on, there are many pieces of connection that hold it together, especially in professional services," Quigley said. "We've got our office and physical plant, our computers and e-mail network, and our telephones and voice-mail network. In the space of ninety minutes we lost our voice-mail network, our computer network, and our office space. We had to put 3,500 people back together and restore laptops, our voice-mail network. We had to restore and create a telephone network and manage communications back to clients, and get those teams functioning."

At Deloitte's board meeting in December 2002, board members elected Quigley to be Deloitte's CEO, a position he resumed officially in June 2003.

"We were out of our office for twelve months," Quigley said. "We didn't lose one client during that time. We had 3,500 people across the street from the towers, literally 100 feet away. I walked away watching those buildings burn and watching people jump out of them. It was a defining moment for me and for our organization."

REFUSE TO LOSE

Less than one week after 9/11, David Neeleman took a train from Connecticut to Washington. He went to the White House to meet with President George Bush. Neeleman and other airline CEOs were there to discuss airport security and passenger safety. Following this White House briefing, Neeleman and his colleagues worked closely with the FAA and other government agencies to craft new security measures throughout the industry.

Within his own company, Neeleman wanted to go further. In the weeks and months following 9/11, he never stopped pushing his employees and his business partners to implement his ideas to upgrade JetBlue security. His persistence paid off. Within a month of 9/11, JetBlue got approval from the FAA to reinforce all cockpit doors with bullet-resistant Kevlar and multiple titanium dead-bolt locks capable of being opened only from within the cockpit.

The security cameras soon followed. Amidst all the new security procedures mandated by the FAA after 9/11, cockpits reinforced with bullet-resistant Kevlar and titanium dead-bolt locks were not among them. Nor were onboard security cameras. To this day, JetBlue is the only airline with these added security features. "We moved on these initiatives voluntarily," Neeleman said.

Neeleman made sure that JetBlue promoted these changes and informed customers in every way possible that their airline was safe. Neeleman attributes this effort, in part, to why JetBlue recovered so quickly. The aftermath of 9/11 caused financial havoc for the airline industry. With financial burdens caused by increased aviation security enhancements and reduction in travel, the major U.S. airlines reported huge losses in 2001 and 2002. Four airlines filed bankruptcy. In contrast, JetBlue had net income of $38.5 million in 2001 and $54.9 million in 2002.

JetBlue even made money in both the third and fourth quarters of 2001, ending up with the highest operating margin of any major U.S. airline during that period. Then on April 11, 2002, exactly six months after 9/11, Morgan Stanley took JetBlue public, selling 6,746,667 shares of common stock at $27 per share. The IPO raised almost $200 million, far exceeding the $150 million the company had anticipated prior to 9/11. And based on its actions in 2001, JetBlue was voted the number-one domestic airline by *Condé Nast Traveler* in 2002.

"I had to be decisive and try to lead and lay out a direction for the future," Neeleman said.

The Neelemans never bought the land they had planned to purchase on 9/11.

NEVER GIVE UP

When Gary Crittenden stepped out of bed on September 12, pains shot up his legs. He could barely walk; his muscles had not recovered from the sprint down forty-seven floors. He went to his private office in his home and participated in a conference call with American Express executives. The company still had not accounted for hundreds of personnel who had worked in the World Trade Center area the day before. There were other problems, too.

The ratings agency S&P had placed American Express on negative watch as a result of the terrorist attack.

Also, the stock market was shut down. When it reopened no one knew what investors would do. If mutual fund holders of American Express Mutual Funds wanted to redeem their positions when the markets reopened, American Express had to be sure it had sufficient cash on hand to meet those demands.

On top of all this, the company had to find new office space for over 3,000 employees in its downtown offices.

Crittenden leaned back in his chair and thought of his decision not to retire a few months earlier.

It wasn't the first time Crittenden had asked himself if what he was doing was worthwhile.

As a nineteen-year-old Mormon missionary, Crittenden had been sent to Germany. At the outset, the experience was filled with frustration and failure. Crittenden was still learning German, and few people had any interest in hearing the missionary message. The winters were long and brutally cold, and Crittenden had to ride a bike everywhere. On top of all this, he was lonesome and homesick.

Then one particularly bitter cold Sunday afternoon, just days before Christmas, he and his missionary companion rode their bikes to Ettlingen, a small rural town near the French border. There they searched for a young college-age student whose name and address had been provided to the missionaries as someone potentially interested in the Church.

After arriving at the apartment building, Crittenden walked around it looking for an entry door. He walked across some boards on the ground, unaware that they covered a deep well. The boards collapsed under his weight. Crittenden cracked through a layer of ice and plunged eight feet down into frigid well water. Wearing a suit and long trench coat, Crittenden struggled to swim up to the surface and hold his head above water. Despite the darkness, he spotted wooden slats on the interior sides of the well and used them to climb out.

His apartment and a dry set of clothes were miles away. His only way back was to pedal his bike. His overcoat froze solid before he reached his apartment. The entire time he pedaled, the question What am I doing here? ran through his mind.

His experience up to that point had been miserable. He was failing to find anyone interested or willing to speak with him about the Mormon faith. He felt like he was completely wasting his time in a faraway foreign land. Meanwhile his colleagues were home attending college or earning money at a job.

Crittenden was ready to abandon his mission and go home. It was Christmastime, after all, and he missed his family. Then that evening he had a life-altering experience. An unprecedented peace and assurance came over him that convinced him he was where he was supposed to be and was doing what he was supposed to be doing. The feeling was so overwhelming that he changed his outlook and his approach. He went on to fulfill his mission and to hold key leadership positions in Germany for the Mormon Church.

"The mission experience was in some ways a pre-play of what

life has been like, at least as far as character development is concerned," Crittenden said. "When you have that experience at a young age and you get through it, you remember that things are never as bad as they feel like on that worst day. And there's always a day when things are going to get better.

"When that day of realization finally comes and you are on your mission for the right reason, it makes all the difference. From then on you get up every morning with an expectation of success and being able to have an influence on people."

Crittenden's Mormon mission experience occurred forty years before 9/11. But the lessons learned there directly influenced his thinking, his approach, and his response to the challenges he and his company faced the morning after.

For the next ten days Crittenden worked out of his home while the company searched for temporary office sites in the Tri-State area. During that time, one of Crittenden's many responsibilities included cutting expenses by reducing about 8,000 American Express employees. He was going over final head counts one September evening at home when he got a call from CEO Ken Chenault. It was 11:00 P.M. Both men had been working almost around the clock for some time. Over the phone that night they made a pact that they would never again be in a position where they didn't have enough flexibility to react to what was going on in the marketplace. They changed their cost structure, their systems, and their processes in the company, enabling American Express to react more quickly to what was happening around them.

As a result of fundamental and wholesale changes within the company, American Express was able to respond rapidly when the SARS epidemic broke out in February 2003. Although the outbreak unexpectedly stopped travel to Asia and triggered negative economic conditions around the world, American Express was able to respond swiftly and without laying off any workers.

Since those difficult days in the wake of 9/11, American Express generated the longest unbroken streak of double-digit growth in earnings of any company in the Dow 30. And American Express recovered from a weak position to where it has the highest PE ratio in the financial services sector and the highest return on capital of any of its competitors. "I like to win," said Crittenden. "I like the feeling of success, particularly when it comes after a long fight, coming off what was truly a difficult situation."

GOING BACK

A year after 9/11, both American Express and Deloitte & Touche had a big decision to make: whether to move back into their offices across the street from Ground Zero. During that time, Gary Crittenden and Jim Quigley talked often.

"There were a lot of good reasons not to go back," Crittenden said. "Everyone in the building on 9/11 had been traumatized. People were scared."

Quigley consulted with private security firms and law enforcement officials, and carefully analyzed and assessed the efforts by city, state, and federal agencies to protect the Wall Street area. Crittenden was evaluating the same risks and security measures for American Express. Other firms headquartered in Lower Manhattan had made the decision to relocate to Midtown. "But the city needed people downtown," Crittenden said. "So we spent a fair amount of time talking about what the right thing was for the city of New York."

Personally, both men agreed they should return to their old office space. Their companies agreed. "We ultimately made the business decision as a commitment to downtown and our very, very strong practice on Wall Street that it would have been a huge statement if we would have pulled out and not gone back," said Quigley. "Frankly, it became a feeling that if we don't go back we are conceding or giving in to these terrorists. We don't want to give in to them. So it was an act of defiance—you are not going to change how we live, how we act, how we think, and how we behave. We just made the business decision."

Some Deloitte employees were so traumatized that they refused to return. "I had some people say, 'I'm not going back. I walked away from here in '93. And I walked away in 2001. I'm not going back inside,'" Quigley said. "I said, 'I understand and respect that. I have a job for you in New Jersey or we'll create an opportunity for you in Connecticut or Long Island.'"

Crittenden admitted feeling apprehensive the first day he returned to the American Express building and reentered his fifty-first-story office nine months after 9/11. He found his laptop right where he'd left it. It was covered with ash and had a metallic smell just like the odor that had permeated the building on 9/11. "I thought at the time of my dad's generation," Crittenden said. "Those guys had to get off of boats and charge the beach. For that generation, that was an incredibly courageous act. For me it felt every bit as courageous to be on the front line of the war on terror, to feel like today may be my last day. But I'm still going to go because somebody has to be here. Somebody has to say that this is okay."

In the year following 9/11, Jim Quigley, Gary Crittenden, and David Neeleman made decisions that dramatically impacted the future of Deloitte & Touche, American Express, and JetBlue Airways. During that same time, Quigley remained the bishop of the New Canaan Mormon Church, where all three men attended church together each Sunday. "They are pretty simple boys," said Bonnie Quigley. "They've come from pretty simple means, not a lot of money or fame or knowledge of the world until they started working in the world. They know who they are. They are comfortable in their own skin. They were taught by humble parents to be good humans, to be humble, to be loyal, and to be good Christians."

CHAPTER 15

THE WALK-AWAY FACTOR

By 2004 Kim Clark was in his ninth year as dean of the Harvard Business School. He had come to the conclusion that ten years is about the right length of service for deans. He shared this with Larry Summers, Harvard's president.

Longtime personal friends, Clark and Summers met in 1976 as graduate students at Harvard, where they studied economics together and went on to publish a series of papers jointly. Summers did not want Clark to leave Harvard. If Clark insisted on stepping down as dean after ten years, Summers wanted to be sure they found another suitable position for him within the university. Clark assured Summers that the only thing that could take him away from Harvard was a call from Salt Lake City. If the Mormon Church asked Clark to serve a full-time service mission or some other assignment, Clark would take it.

Over the next year, Clark and his wife, Sue, started discussing what Kim should do after completion of his time as dean. The idea of working somewhere other than Harvard seemed remote. Only one job away from Cambridge stood out: president of Brigham Young University in Provo, Utah. BYU is the Mormon Church's flagship campus. The chance to run it had always seemed appealing to Clark. But that job was not available.

While the Clarks were having discussions about Kim's future, the president of BYU-Idaho was called to be a member of the Quorum of Twelve Apostles in the Church of Jesus Christ of Latter-day Saints. In 2001 the Church had converted its two-year junior college in Idaho known as Ricks College into a four-year institution and renamed it Brigham Young University-Idaho. Before the fall of 2004 the idea of going to Idaho never crossed Clark's mind. The Idaho campus was new, much smaller, and lacked the reputation of BYU in Utah. Going from Harvard to BYU-Idaho would certainly not be viewed in academia as a move up.

Yet the more Clark thought about the opportunities and the challenges presented by the job in Idaho, the more intrigued with the idea he became. What if am asked to preside over BYU-Idaho? he asked himself. What would I do?

By spring of 2005, Clark convinced himself it would be an exciting and great challenge to take the reins at BYU-Idaho. He even told his wife that he would likely take the job if it was offered. But it wasn't. The Church never called.

With his tenure as dean at HBS now pushing the ten-year mark, Clark started feeling unsettled, even a bit anxious about what he ought to do after his time as dean was over. As was their habit, the Clarks began praying about this question. On May 25, 2005, as soon as dinner ended, Kim cleaned up the kitchen while Sue retrieved a slew of voice-mail messages from the telephone.

Most of them were not urgent. Suddenly, Sue stopped. "Kim, this one you better listen to," she said.

"Who is it?" he asked.

"It's from Salt Lake," she said, handing him the phone.

The message was from the executive secretary for Gordon B. Hinckley, the president and prophet of the Mormon Church.

Clark stepped into the living room and called President Hinckley's secretary, who informed Clark that Hinckley had left the office. The secretary told Clark it would be cruel, however, to make him wait until the following day. He asked Clark to hold on while he attempted to reach President Hinckley.

Less than a minute later President Hinckley came on the line and greeted Clark. "Now, Brother Clark," Clark recalled him saying, "this is not a calling. I just want to explore this with you. This is exploratory."

Hinckley asked Clark how long he would remain at HBS and about his future plans. Then he asked Clark if he would be interested in presiding over BYU-Idaho. Clark didn't hesitate. "I would," he said.

They briefly discussed the school and its strengths.

"Can you get there by fall?" Hinckley asked.

"I can."

Hinckley encouraged Clark to talk it over with Sue, pray about it, and consider a fall date. "Think along those lines," he said.

After hanging up with President Hinckley, Clark talked with his wife. But there was really little to discuss. "When you pray to the Lord and say, 'Help me know what to do,'" said Clark, "and the person who calls is the prophet of the Lord, it doesn't get any clearer than that. It doesn't get any clearer."

The next day Clark called President Hinckley back.

"We'd love to do it if that's what you want us to do," Clark said.

"Good," the prophet said. "Can you come in the fall?"

"We can."

"Well, all right. We'll consider this matter settled."

President Hinckley had shaken hands with Clark on one prior occasion. They had never had a conversation before the phone call. No résumé was submitted, and no job interview was conducted. In a matter of two phone calls lasting less than half an hour in total, BYU-Idaho had a new college president and Harvard Business School needed a new dean.

After hanging up with President Hinckley, Clark called Larry Summers at his Harvard office. "Larry, the phone call we thought might come has come," Clark told him. "I got a call from President Hinckley last night. They want me to be president of BYU-Idaho."

Summers could not believe the suddenness of the decision. But he did not try to talk Clark out of it. Instead, he and Clark started planning Clark's departure announcement.

A day later, President Hinckley and Clark spoke again by phone.

"Now, Brother Clark, are you settled in your mind on this?"

"Yes, I am. There's no doubt."

"Good."

Harvard, BYU-Idaho, and the Mormon Church worked collectively on a complicated plan to announce Clark's resignation at HBS and his hiring at BYU-Idaho. On May 31, 2005, Clark told his closest staff of his decision. A week later, on June 6, an e-mail went out to all HBS faculty, announcing a special faculty meeting at twelve-thirty that afternoon. Faculty meetings are typically calendared a year in advance. This time people had four hours' notice, sending a signal that something big was happening. Nearly 150 faculty showed up in an oversized room on campus. Summers and Clark entered the room together.

"I called this meeting so I could announce my resignation, effective July thirty-first," said Clark, informing them he had accepted the position as president of BYU-Idaho. The faculty was stunned. Clark pointed to a chair at the head of the room. "Ten years ago when I was named dean I sat right in that chair," he said. That day Harvard's former president Neil Rudenstein introduced Clark as the business school's new dean. "At that time I said two things," Clark continued. "One was that I love the school and I'm grateful for the opportunity. Two, in my judgment we were only limited by our imagination.

"Ten years later, I believe both of those things continue to be true. But I would add one more that I've learned in the last ten years: If we work together and pull together, there really is no limit to what we can do. So two things remain true: I love the school and I still think we are only limited by our imagination. And if we work together there is no limit to what we can do."

After Clark spoke to his faculty, Summers addressed them. Then Clark went to a media room on campus, where he was linked by satellite with Gordon B. Hinckley, who was in Salt Lake City. Speaking by satellite to nearly 10,000 students gathered on campus at BYU-Idaho, Hinckley announced the appointment of Clark as the school's new president. The students cheered. Clark spoke to them via satellite from Harvard.

As soon as Clark finished, he and Summers attended a press conference at the business school. Summers told the Boston press that Clark's departure would create a big hole at the business school. "Kim Clark will be very, very much missed," Summers told the press. When Clark took over as dean, the school's endowment has been $550 million. In ten years he led the fund-raising effort to more than triple it to $2.1 billion. He invested in technology and opened HBS research centers in others parts of the world. He increased faculty by 20 percent, and in the wake of the corporate scandals, he instituted new courses of instruction on ethics.

A reporter asked Summers if he had attempted to change Clark's mind about going to Idaho.

"It became clear to me I was the president of Harvard," Summers replied. "And the president of Kim's church had spoken."

When Clark addressed the press, he acknowledged how much he would miss Harvard. "If the president of my church had not called me on the twenty-fifth of May, we would not be here," he said. "I have been very happy being the dean of our business school. I think it's one of the great jobs in the world, and I love this university."

As soon as the press conference adjourned, Clark and his wife rushed to the airport, boarded a private plane, and flew directly to Idaho, arriving that night. The following morning Clark addressed the student body and then hopped back on a plane and returned to Boston that afternoon to prepare for commencement ceremonies the following day. In his commencement speech, Clark told the graduates he wanted to share with them a principle and some advice.

"First the principle," he said, asking them to reflect for a moment on leadership. "If you turn around, you will see seated and standing behind you some very remarkable people."

The graduates turned around and faced their parents, partners, friends, and family.

"In your time at HBS you have read many cases and studied many companies," Clark said. "One thing I hope you have learned is that no company can compete successfully unless it builds on a strong foundation. For you as individuals, there will be no more secure foundation in your life than a home that is full of life and love. Conversely—I hope you listen carefully to what I am going to say—you will find no success in business that can compensate for failure in the home. Let me say that one more time. Take these words to heart, listen to me, because these are true words, this is a true principle: There is no success in business that can compensate for failure at home.

"But there is no success without investment. That's another lesson I know you have learned. If you are going to be successful, you have to invest. So I encourage you to invest first at home and to think of this as by far your most important investment. Indeed, I believe that the most important work that you will do in your lives will be within the walls of your own home. So that's my principle for you."

Next Clark gave the advice. "When you walk from this place today with diploma in hand you will be a graduate of the Harvard Business School. A world of opportunities—opportunities many people can't even imagine—lies before you. In the course of your lives and careers, you are likely to be blessed with power—and with the privilege and wealth that come with it. I know this may sound like a really good thing, but it comes with significant risk to you, and to those you love.

"So here is my advice: Don't let it get into your heart. Don't let wealth and privilege and power become ends in themselves, and a corrosive force in your life. Don't set your heart on them. Set your heart on being a person of integrity, the kind of person whose values offer strength and purpose to those around them. Be the kind of person that others will trust with their lives."

Clark finished with a request. "We need leaders who will make a difference in the world," he said, "leaders who are firmly grounded in the highest standards of integrity and respect and personal accountability, leaders who are not afraid to set their sights high, who will dream and hope and believe in themselves and in those around them."

Days before Kim Clark left Harvard Business School, I conducted a final interview with him at his office. I asked him what he and these other Mormon executives have in common. He asked for a few moments to think and then offered these three ideas.

First: *They each grew up in the culture of the Mormon Church.* "Growing up in that culture places a strong emphasis on the importance of gaining knowledge and seeking as much education and advancement as you can in your life," Clark said.

Second: *A mandate to be in the world, but not of the world.* "This notion of excelling in the world is deep in the Mormon culture and goes way, way back to the pioneers," Clark said. "Brigham Young and Joseph Smith had a desire to be excellent in what they did. There was this drive in the world's terms to be great at music, mathematics, and engineering, build beautiful cities and great buildings. Growing up there's this cultural mandate to seek knowledge and excellence in what you do and become very good at it. Living your faith in the world means engaging the world. It is not being apart from the world."

Third: *Growing up in the Mormon Church teaches you how to be a leader.* "If you take advantage of it—not all Mormon youth do—there are lots of incredibly powerful developmental experiences that are unusual, starting when you are twelve," Clark said. "You get to be a leader. You learn how to plan, organize, direct others, and motivate. From the time you are twelve you have about ten years of these experiences. You grow up in a church that is built on the leadership of its members, not on a cadre of elite people. As a result, if you have any kind of natural ability along these lines, you get developed and these leadership instincts mature."

There are many things that distinguish these CEOs from others. Most of them delayed schooling and gave up two years of their life at age nineteen to serve full-time missions for their church. All of them give 10 percent of their income in tithing. None of them consume alcohol or tobacco. They serve in substantial church leadership positions on top of their corporate responsibilities. And they are fiercely loyal to their spouses and families. But perhaps the most unusual aspect to them is that at some point they will walk away from their positions of power in the business world to serve full time in some non-compensated church capacity. Kim Clark's position is a paid position in a church-owned university, but many successful Mormon corporate leaders have retired to serve service missions with their wives or to respond to calls from the Mormon Church's president, Gordon B. Hinckley, to serve as General Authorities.

After such a prestigious career in the corporate world, a full-time, non-compensated ecclesiastical leadership position is certainly not the normal retirement plan in corporate America. Yet when asked, every executive interviewed for this book said he is willing to walk away from the corporate world and serve full time for the Mormon Church if or when called to do so. "We realize that success in this life is not what will get us ahead," said Dell CEO Kevin Rollins. "This is part of a course to an end, not an end in and of itself. Most of us would give it all up immediately for something higher. I would because if it's right I can get it again. It's like Job in the Old Testament: If God wants you to have it, you'll get it again. If he doesn't, you won't."

Although all of the CEOs in this book said they would walk away to serve in a full-time church capacity if asked, they all expressed a strong belief that now is not the time for such a move. "If the Lord says he wants me to go do a service mission in Chile," said Kevin Rollins, "I would do it today. But I don't think it would be right today. I consider my job now, while it is very important to the world, it is not very important to God. What's particularly important to God is that while I'm visible in the world that I behave appropriately. I think in this position I have a responsibility: Do not screw up, do not goof up, do not misbehave."

David Neeleman is not ready to leave business yet, either. "The thing that keeps me here isn't money," Neeleman said. "I really feel indebted to our crew members who work here. As the creator of JetBlue, I'd be letting them down if I walked away right now. And I'm young and get a great deal of satisfaction doing what I'm doing."

When Neeleman does walk away, he won't head toward retirement. "When I do finally go, the idea of going to Florida to play golf or bridge is not even in the realm of my thinking," he said. Instead, he looks forward to a mission of service. "Unless you are serving others or helping lift others, you can't reach your full measure of happiness in this life."

None of these CEOs presume they will be called or asked by the Church to do anything. But all of them are willing to volunteer one day to serve full time in a church capacity. "The reason we would all do it," said Kevin Rollins, "is because we realize that what we're doing in the business world is a good thing. But it's not the best thing. There's a higher good. I firmly believe that when we leave this life, the things we are doing and the positions we held will not matter much. God is not going to care very much about that. He is going to care about other things you did to help people, to improve people. I believe that to my bones."

This approach, more than anything, explains why these leaders approach their roles as CEOs the way they do. Of course they take their corporate responsibilities very seriously. But they know their corporate roles are temporary and that when life ends, wealth and titles won't matter. "The perspective is that what you are doing now is not quite as important as you think it is, or as important as others think it is . . . because it will go away," said Kevin Rollins. "The prominence, the money, the power, and the titles will all be stripped away. Then what are you? It's then that I want to be something."

ACKNOWLEDGMENTS

Not often does an author make so many genuine friends when working on a book. The richest aspect of this project may be the relationships I've forged with the individuals whose lives and habits I've chronicled in these pages. They inspired me to change and improve. I thank David and Vicki Neeleman, Dave and Deb Checketts, Jim and Bonnie Quigley, Kevin and Debbie Rollins, Gary and Cathy Crittenden, Rod and Beverly Hawes, Kim and Sue Clark, and Clayton and Christine Christensen. Thank you for allowing me into your homes. Thank you for permitting me to climb into your pasts. And thank you for your trust.

Don Staheli was a priceless source of guidance and wisdom. He was a stranger when I began this book. Now he is a trusted friend and mentor.

JetBlue, Madison Square Garden, Dell, Deloitte & Touche, American Express, Harvard Business School, and Brigham Young University-Idaho were most cooperative and helpful. In particular, the executive assistants for the CEOs featured in the book were resourceful, prompt, and thorough in ways that made my job easier. They are Carol Archer, Clare Gluck, JaNeece Watkins, April Neuhaus, Ava Sloane, Deborah McNair, Susan Deavor, and Alice Ann Weber. This quiet, less visible group knows how to get things done and makes things happen that are vital to the success of their employers.

ACKNOWLEDGMENTS

The less visible key to my success is my wife, Lydia. Besides her ever steady presence in our home, she provided crucial editing and shaping on the chapter about women. My sons Tennyson and Clancy (nine and five, respectively, at the time this book was researched) were great traveling companions. They accompanied me to JetBlue's offices and to the homes of various CEOs for interviews. My daughters Maggie May and Clara Belle are too young to realize the inspiration they provided.

My personal assistant, Donna Cochrane, is the perfect professional: resourceful, prompt, spirited, and contagiously happy.

My editor, Rick Wolff, is the visionary behind this project. He deserves the credit for the idea. My agent, Basil Kane, was involved at every crucial step of the way.

Clark Gilbert at the Harvard Business School offered top-shelf marketing and sales ideas.

INDEX

acquisitions, *see* mergers and
  acquisitions
Airbus, 79, 173, 182, 195
Alberta, Rollins's mission in, 9
alcohol, avoidance of, 58–63, 129,
  215
American Express, x, xii, 20, 56, 62,
  66–68, 103
  and aftermath of 9/11, 67–68,
    201, 203–6
  and Crittenden's avoidance of
    infidelity, 67–68
  Crittenden's competitiveness and,
    34–35
  Crittenden's religious
    commitments and, 49
  finances of, 81, 113, 201, 203–4
  9/11 terrorist attacks and, 170–72,
    178–79, 185–86, 189
  prioritizing time commitments
    and, 113, 115–18
  Sabbath and, 129, 131
  SARS epidemic and, 203–4
  trust and, 81
American Motors Corporation
  (AMC), 44, 59
Archer, Carol, xii
Arthur Andersen, 65

Bain, Bill, 110–11
Bain & Company, 35, 41, 50, 86,
  110, 113
Boeing, 79–80
Boston Consulting Group (BCG),
  141–42
Brazil, Neeleman's mission in, 4
Brigham Young University (BYU),
  8–10, 15, 24, 72, 77
  Idaho campus of, 208–12, 215
  wives' education at, 147–48
Bunker, Edward, 92
Bush, George, 199
Bush, Jeb, 136–37
business plans, business models, 25–26
  Crittenden's competitiveness and,
    34–35
Butts, Earl, 148

Cablevision Systems Corp., 15, 107,
  127, 133
Cantor Fitzgerald, 191
Checketts, Dave, xii, 12–24
  childhood and adolescence of,
    12–15, 86–87, 165
  competitiveness of, 15–16, 22–24,
    26–34, 37
  daily prayer habit of, 55

Checketts, Dave (*cont.*)
daily scripture study of, 55
education of, 15, 28
family life of, 12–14, 27, 30, 34,
58, 62, 87, 110–11, 126–28,
132–34, 165
finances of, 34, 87, 110–11
mission of, 1, 12, 14–16, 19–21, 105
mother's influence on, 165
motivations of, 19, 37
negotiations of, 17–19, 27–32
on persistence, 12–14, 16, 20
power and, 101, 104–11
profanity avoided by, 62
religious beliefs and commitments
of, 1, 15, 19, 26, 37, 105,
126–27, 165
Sabbath and, 125–29, 165
trust and, 80, 83–85
and wife as stay-at-home mother,
146, 151, 154–56, 158–59
Checketts, Debbie, 17, 27, 107, 128,
133, 166
daily prayer habit of, 55
as stay-at-home mother, 146, 151,
154–56, 158–59
Checketts, Elizabeth, 133–34
Checketts, Katie, 111
Chenault, Ken, 113
and aftermath of 9/11, 203
9/11 terrorist attacks and, 170–71
China, Dell's penetration into,
35–36, 138
Christensen, Clayton, xii
education of, 19, 140–41
family life of, 138–43
mission of, 19–20
motivation and, 19–20
Sabbath and, 141–42
Church of Jesus Christ of Latter-day
Saints, *see* Mormons, Mormon

Church, Mormonism
Clark, Kim, xii, 207–15
adult children of, 166–67
author's interview with, xviii–xxi
childhood of, xix–x, 90–92,
163–65
competition and, xviii, xx
on culture of Mormon Church,
214–15
daily scripture study of, 56–57
departure from HBS of, 207–13
education of, 11, 119, 163–65, 207
family life of, xix–xx, 51–52,
90–91, 93, 119–22, 138,
163–65
finances of, 88, 90–92, 215
HBS commencement speech of,
212–14
heritage of, 92
leisure activities and, 51
management skills of, xx, 11–12,
164–65
mission of, 10–12
mother's influence on, xx, 163–65
power and, 99–100, 104, 106
and principle of stewardship,
92–93
prioritizing time commitments
and, 112, 118–22, 124
religious beliefs and commitments
of, xix, 88, 91–92, 120, 122,
164, 207–9, 212, 214–15
and wife as stay-at-home mother,
150, 154–55, 168–69
Clark, Merlin, 90–91
Clark, Sue, 51–52, 138, 165–67
adult children of, 166–67
and husband's departure from
HBS, 207–9, 212
prioritizing time commitments
and, 119–22

as stay-at-home mother, 150, 154–55, 165–66, 168–69

coffee, avoidance of, 59–60

commitments, prioritizing of, 112–24, 137

competition, competitors, competitiveness, 22–35, 173, 204, 213
  of Checketts, 15–16, 22–24, 26–34, 37
  Clark and, xviii, xx
  of Crittenden, 34–35
  JetBlue and, 25
  Neeleman and, xiii, 22–24
  Quigley's religious commitments and, 48
  of Rollins, 22, 27
  success and, 28–30, 34–35
  trust and, 72

consistency, 11

Continental Grain Company, x, 44–47

corporate scandals, 70–72, 81, 95–96, 100

Crittenden, Cathy, 50–52, 58, 66–68, 112–13
  adult children of, 162, 166, 185–86, 190
  finances of, 89–90, 148–49
  9/11 terrorist attacks and, 171, 179, 185–86, 190
  prioritizing time commitments and, 116, 118
  as stay-at-home mother, 146, 148–49, 156, 159–60, 162

Crittenden, Gary, xii, 200–206
  adult children of, 162, 166, 185–86, 190
  and aftermath of 9/11, 67–68, 200–201, 203–6
  alcohol avoided by, 62
  competitiveness of, 34–35

daily prayer habit of, 54

daily scripture study of, 56–57

education of, 50–51, 89, 148, 159

family life of, 50–52, 58, 67–68, 113–16, 118, 148–49, 159–60

finances of, 89–90, 94, 148, 189–90

infidelity avoided by, 66–69

leisure activities and, 51–52

mission of, 20, 112–13, 201–3

motivation and, 49–50

9/11 terrorist attacks and, 170–71, 178–79, 185–87, 189–90, 201

persistence of, 20

power and, 103

prioritizing time commitments and, 113–18

religious beliefs and commitments of, 49–52, 89–90, 103, 113–14, 117–18, 159, 206

retirement considered by, 112–13

Sabbath and, 131

trust and, 81

and wife as stay-at-home mother, 146, 148–49, 156, 159–60, 162

Crittenden, Stephanie, 166
  9/11 terrorist attacks and, 185–86, 190

customers, xiii, 23–25, 139
  and aftermath of 9/11, 194, 196, 198, 200
  and avoidance of infidelity, 66–67
  Neeleman's management style and, 1–2, 4
  9/11 terrorist attacks and, 174, 181, 188
  trust and, 82

Davis, Martin, 33

deference, power and, 101

delegation, 196–98

Dell, Michael, 7, 35, 41–44
  power and, 98–99
Dell Inc., x–xi, xviii, 19, 41–44, 166,
    215
  corporate culture of, 123
  family life and, 134–35, 137
  finances of, 41–43, 82–83, 86
  power and, 98–99, 101–2
  prioritizing time commitments
    and, 112, 122–23
  and Rollins's avoidance of
    infidelity, 69
  Rollins's management skills and, 7,
    43–44, 82–83, 163
  Rollins's preparation and, 35–36
  Rollins's religious commitments
    and, 41–43
  Sabbath and, 129
  trust and, 73–74, 82–83
Deloitte & Touche USA, x–xii,
    38–41, 46–49
  and aftermath of 9/11, 194–99,
    204–6
  and finances, 72, 96
  and 9/11 terrorist attacks, 43,
    171–72, 174–78, 180, 183–84,
    186–91, 194
  and power, 102
  and Quiqley's avoidance of
    alcohol, 60–61
  and Quigley's avoidance of
    infidelity, 65–66
  and Quigley's management skills,
    43, 47–49, 196–97
  and Quigley's religious
    commitments, 39–41, 43, 46, 49
  and trust, 70–72, 81–82
Disney, 12, 16–17, 27, 125–26
divorce, divorces, 66–67, 140
Dolan, Jim, 133–34
Drucker, Peter, 5, 23

East Los Angeles, Calif., Checketts's
    mission in, 14–16
Ebbers, Bernard J., 70, 96
Eisner, Michael, 125–26
Eli Lilly, xii, 19
employees, xiii, xv, xviii, 216
  and aftermath of 9/11, 67,
    197–98, 201, 203–5
  Clark's daily scripture study and, 56
  Clark's management style and, 12
  and Crittenden's avoidance of
    infidelity, 67
  Crittenden's religious
    commitments and, 49
  family life and, 135–36, 141–42
  finances and, 96
  and Neeleman's avoidance of
    alcohol, 61
  Neeleman's management style and,
    2–6
  9/11 terrorist attacks and, 171–78,
    181–84, 186–91, 194, 199
  power and, 102, 104–9
  prioritizing time commitments
    and, 116, 121
  Quigley's management skills and,
    43, 49
  Sabbath and, 125, 130–31
  trust and, 76–78, 82
Enron, 70, 81, 100
Evans, Dick, 27
Ewing, Patrick, 83
  Checketts's competitiveness and,
    28–33

face time, power and, 100
Falk, David, 28–30, 32
family, family life, 105–6, 215
  avoiding infidelity and, 68–69
  of Checketts, 12–14, 27, 30, 34,
    58, 62, 87, 110–11, 126–28,
    132–34, 165

of Christensen, 138–43
of Clark, xix–xx, 51–52, 90–91,
   93, 119–22, 138, 163–65
Clark's HBS commencement
   speech and, 212–13
of Crittenden, 50–52, 58, 67–68,
   113–16, 118, 148–49, 159–60
daily prayer habit and, 54–56
daily scripture study and, 55–56
eternality of, 109–11
finances and, 87, 90–91, 94–95
of Hawes, 74, 77, 124, 129–30,
   152, 160–61
leisure activities and, 51–52
of Neeleman, xiii, xv–xvi, 20–21,
   51, 68, 87, 95, 97, 110,
   130–32, 135–37, 145,
   157–58
9/11 terrorist attacks and, 184
power and, 102, 109–11
prioritizing time commitments
   and, 112–16, 118–24, 137
as priority, 132–43
of Quigley, 38–40, 46, 51–52, 58,
   102, 149–50
regular vacations with, 58, 95
of Rollins, 7–10, 42–43, 54, 58,
   69, 110, 112, 123, 134–35,
   137–38, 162–63
Sabbath and, 125–31, 141–42
of Staheli, 45
see also wives
Federal Reserve Bank, 44
Ferraro, Henry, 177
firing employees, 106–9
Fortune, 44
Freda, Bill:
   and aftermath of 9/11, 198
   9/11 terrorist attacks and, 172,
      174–75, 180, 187–88
free agency, 60
Fribourg, Michel, 45

General Mills, Inc., 44
Germany:
   Clark's mission in, 10–11
   Crittenden's mission in, 20, 201–3
Golden State Warriors, 29, 31–32, 34
Goldman Sachs, 62
Grunfeld, Ernie, 84
   firing of, 107–9

habit, habits, 53–69, 163
   avoiding alcohol and, 58–63, 129,
      215
   avoiding infidelity and, 59, 64–69,
      129, 215
   avoiding profanity and, 59, 62–63
   of daily prayer, 53–56
   of daily scripture study, 54–57
   prioritizing time commitments
      and, 118
   regular family vacations as, 58, 95
Hart, Gary, 148
Harvard Business School (HBS),
      ix–x, xviii–xx, 10–12, 75–77,
      88–89, 150, 166–67, 207–14
   Christensen's time at, xii, 19,
      138–41, 143
   Clark's commencement speech at,
      212–14
   Clark's daily scripture study and, 56
   Clark's departure from, 207–13
   Clark's finances and, 88, 91
   Clark's management skills and,
      11–12, 164
   Clark's stewardship and, 92–93
   Crittenden's time at, 50–51, 89,
      148, 159
   finances of, xix, 119, 212
   Hawes's time at, 75, 152, 160
   power and, 99
   prioritizing time commitments
      and, 112, 118–22
   Sabbath and, 129–30

Hawes, Beverly, 124, 151–52
    adult children of, 168
    as stay-at-home mother, 152, 154,
        160–61, 167–68
Hawes, Rod, xii, 151–52
    adult children of, 168
    childhood of, 74, 77
    education of, 74–75, 160
    fame of, 76–77
    family life of, 74, 77, 124, 129–30,
        152, 160–61
    finances of, 74
    heritage of, 74
    management skills of, 47
    prioritizing time commitments
        and, 123–24
    Quigley's relationship with, 46–48
    religious beliefs and commitments
        of, xvii, 46, 48, 74–75, 152
    Sabbath and, 125, 129–30
    trust and, 74–77
    and wife as stay-at-home mother,
        152, 154, 160–61, 167–68
Hewlett-Packard, 25
Hinckley, Gordon B., 94–95,
    209–12, 215

"If" (Kipling), 30
Imus, Don, 55
infidelity:
    avoidance of, 59, 64–69, 129, 215
    divorce and, 66–67
inner circle, power and, 99–100
Innovator's Dilemma, The
    (Christensen), 138
insubordination, power and, 106
Intel, xii, 19
investors, 113, 181
    family life and, 136
    JetBlue's finances and, 94
    trust and, 77–78, 80

ITT, 15–16, 127

Jackson, Phil, 83–85
JetBlue Airways Corp., x–xv, 23, 37,
    77–80, 130–32, 147, 154,
    157–58, 172–74, 216
    and aftermath of 9/11, 195–96,
        199–200, 206
    family life and, 136–37
    finances of, xiii, 25, 94, 136,
        172–73, 181–82, 187–88, 200
    and Neeleman's avoidance of
        alcohol, 61
    Neeleman's management skills and,
        xiii, 1–6, 25, 187–88
    9/11 terrorist attacks and, 174,
        178, 180–82, 187–88, 191–92
    power and, 102, 110
    Sabbath and, 125, 130–31
    trust and, 78–80
Jones, Dan, 38–40

Kelly, Tom, 173, 187, 191
Kipling, Rudyard, 30
Kodak, xii, 19
Korea, Christensen's mission in, 19
Kozlowski, Dennis, 95–96

leisure activities, family life and,
    51–52, 146
Life Re Corporation, xii, 74, 125,
    129–30
    finances of, 47, 76
    Hawes's management skills and, 47
    Sabbath and, 130
    trust and, 76
Los Angeles Lakers, 33
Lustgarten, Marc, 107

Madison Square Garden (MSG)
    Corp., x, xii, 1, 12, 15–19, 155
    acquistions of, 16–19, 127

Checketts's competitiveness and, 27, 33
family life and, 132–34
finances of, 15–16, 18–19, 129
power and, 104–9
Sabbath and, 125, 127–29
markets, 35–36, 138, 173, 203
Marriott, J. Willard, Jr. "Bill," ix, 53
Marriott, J. Willard, Sr., 44, 53
Marriott International Inc., 44, 53
MCI:
    finances of, 96
    trust and, 70–72
mergers and acquisitions, 152, 166, 168, 190
    of MSG, 16–19, 127
    and Open Skies, 25
    and prioritizing time commitments, 123–24
    and Quigley's avoidance of infidelity, 66
    and trust, 75–77
Mitsubishi Estates, 16–18
Morgan Stanley, 166, 172–73, 181, 185, 200
Mormons, Mormon Church, Mormonism:
    of author, ix
    culture of, 214–15
    finances of, 10–11, 39, 46, 87–97, 129, 215
    in history, xvii, 36–37, 87–88, 92, 146, 214
    missionary program of, 1, 3–4, 6–7, 9–12, 14–16, 19–21, 105, 112–13, 138, 147, 156, 185, 201–3, 215–16
    rules and traditions of, x–xi, xvii–xviii, 3, 6, 26, 38–52, 54–57, 60, 63–64, 68, 109–11, 120, 126, 128–29, 132,

134–35, 141, 165, 184–85, 187–88
Morris Air, 23–25, 157–58
    trust and, 77–78
motivations, motivators, 26
    of Checketts, 19, 37
    Christensen and, 19–20
    Crittenden's religious commitments and, 49–50
    of Neeleman, xiii, 23–24, 37
    power and, 99–100
    Quigley's management skills and, 49
    in success, 22–23
Mullin, Chris, 29, 34
Mutual of New York, 75

National Institute for Child Health and Human Development, 151, 162
NBA International, 27
Neeleman, David, xi–xvi, 1–7, 172–74
    ADD of, 6, 24
    adult children of, 167
    and aftermath of 9/11, 195–96, 199–200, 205–6
    alcohol avoided by, 61
    author's interview with, xii–xv
    book CDs of, xv, 56–57
    childhood and adolescence of, 5–6
    competition and, xiii, 22–24
    daily prayer habit of, 55–56
    daily scripture study of, 55–57
    education of, 5–6, 147
    family life of, xiii, xv–xvi, 20–21, 51, 68, 87, 95, 97, 110, 130–32, 135–37, 145, 157–58
    finances of, 5, 25, 87–88, 94–95, 97
    infidelity avoided by, 68
    leisure activities and, 51

Neeleman, David (*cont.*)
  management style of, xiii–xiv, 1–6,
    25, 187–88
  mission of, 1, 3–4, 6–7, 147
  motivations of, xiii, 23–24, 37
  9/11 terrorist attacks and, 173–74,
    177–78, 180–82, 185, 187–88,
    191–92, 200
  power and, 102, 110
  profanity avoided by, 62
  on readiness to leave business, 216
  religious beliefs and commitments
    of, xiii–xv, 3–4, 26, 37, 94–95,
    97, 131, 206
  Sabbath and, 125, 130–31
  trust and, 77–80
  and wife as stay-at-home mother,
    145–47, 149, 154, 156–58,
    161–62, 169
Neeleman, Vicki Vranes, xv, 68, 95,
    97, 173
  adult children of, 167
  daily scripture study of, 55
  9/11 terrorist attacks and, 177–78,
    187, 191–92, 200
  as stay-at-home mother, 145–47,
    149, 154, 156–58, 161–62, 169
negotiations, negotiating, 189
  Checketts's competitiveness and,
    27–32
  and Quigley's avoidance of
    infidelity, 66
  Radio City Productions deal and,
    17–19
  Rollins's preparation and, 36
  Sabbath and, 127
  trust and, 79–80
New York Knicks, 15, 55
  Checketts's competitiveness and,
    27–33
  family life and, 132

power and, 104, 107–9
Sabbath and, 126–28
trust and, 83–84
New York Rangers, 15, 55
  power and, 104–6
  Sabbath and, 127–28
9/11 terrorist attacks, 43, 166,
    170–92
  aftermath of, 67–68, 194–201,
    203–6
  casualties in, 176, 185–86, 191, 199
  evacuations in, 174–79, 182–83,
    185

obedience, relationship between
    success and, 9
Open Skies, 25
Owen, John, 173

Paramount, 33
partners, partnerships, xiii, xviii,
    38–41
  and aftermath of 9/11, 196
  9/11 terrorist attacks and, 172,
    175–77, 180, 183–84, 186–90
  power and, 103
  and Quigley's avoidance of alcohol,
    61
  Quigley's management skills and, 49
  and Quigley's religious
    commitments, 39–41
  Rollins's preparation and, 36
  trust and, 76, 79
PE ratios, 204
persistence:
  of Checketts, 12–14, 16, 20
  of Crittenden, 20
Pop Shoppe, 9–10, 41
  trust and, 72–73
power, 23, 98–111, 213, 217
  family life and, 102, 109–11

firing employees and, 106–9
Mormon bishops on, 103–5
Rollins and, 98–99, 101–2, 110
trappings of, 99–102
prayer, 69, 191, 208–9
as daily habit, 53–56
preferential treatment, power and,
100–102
preparation, success and, 35–36
prioritizing time commitments,
112–24, 137
products, production, productivity,
xx, 19
family life and, 135–36, 142
prioritizing time commitments
and, 121
and Quigley's avoidance of
infidelity, 65
trust and, 72
profanity:
avoidance of, 59, 62–63
sexual harassment and, 63
profits, profitability, 42, 139, 168

Quigley, Bonnie, 38–40, 46, 51–52,
206
adult children of, 58, 168, 185,
188
9/11 terrorist attacks and, 175,
184–85, 188, 190–91
as stay-at-home mother, 145,
149–50, 161
Quigley, Jim, xi–xii, 193–99
adult children of, 58, 168, 185,
188
and aftermath of 9/11, 194–99,
204–6
alcohol avoided by, 60–61
childhood and adolescence of,
149, 193–94
competitiveness of, 48

education of, 49, 149
family life of, 38–40, 46, 51–52,
58, 102, 149–50
finances and, 40, 95–96
Hawes's relationship with, 46–48
infidelity avoided by, 64–66
leisure activities and, 51–52
management skills of, 43, 47–49,
196–97
mother's influence on, 194
motivation and, 49
9/11 terrorist attacks and, 43,
171–72, 174–77, 180, 183–91,
194, 199
power and, 102–4, 106–7
religious beliefs and commitments
of, 38–41, 43–44, 46–49,
95–96, 103–4, 184, 191, 206
Staheli's relationship with, 44,
46–48
trust and, 70–72, 81–82
and wife as stay-at-home mother,
145, 149–50, 161
Quigley, Morgan, 9/11 terrorist
attacks and, 185, 188

Rabin, Yitzhak, 127
Radio City Music Hall, 128
MSG's acquisition of, 16–19
Riley, Pat, Checketts's
competitiveness and, 28–30,
32–33
Rockefeller Center, 16–18
Rollins, Debbie, 9–10, 58, 69, 123,
135, 138, 147–49
adult children of, 167
husband's religious commitments
and, 42–43
as stay-at-home mother, 149, 153
Rollins, Kevin, xi, xviii, 53–55, 147–49
adult children of, 167

Rollins, Kevin (*cont.*)
  beverage business of, 9–10, 41, 72–73
  childhood of, 7–9, 54, 162–63
  competitiveness of, 22, 27
  daily prayer habit of, 54–55
  daily scripture study of, 57
  education of, 8–10, 72, 162–63
  family life of, 7–10, 42–43, 54, 58, 69, 110, 112, 123, 134–35, 137–38, 162–63
  finances of, 9, 86, 88
  infidelity avoided by, 69
  management style of, 7, 9–10, 43–44, 82–83, 163
  mission of, 7, 9
  mother's influence on, 162–63
  motivations of, 23
  power and, 98–99, 101–2, 110
  preparation of, 35–36
  prioritizing time commitments and, 112, 122–23, 137
  on readiness to leave business, 216–17
  religious beliefs and commitments of, 9, 41–43, 73, 112, 123, 215–17
  trust and, 72–74, 82–83
  and wife as stay-at-home mother, 149, 153
Romney, George W., 44, 59
Romney, Mitt, ix
Rudenstein, Neil, 211

Sabbath, 165
  challenges presented by, 129–30
  family life and, 125–31, 141–42
  flexibility on, 125, 129–31
  prioritizing time commitments and, 120, 123
sales, salesmanship, selling, 19, 75

  and Quigley's avoidance of infidelity, 65
  trust and, 82
SARS epidemic, 203–4
scripture study, 128
  as daily habit, 54–57
Securities and Exchange Commission (SEC), 71, 181–82
self-importance, power and, 101–2
service, xiii, 25
  and aftermath of 9/11, 194, 196
  Neeleman's management style and, 1–3
sexual harassment, 63, 108
Sloane, Ava, 9/11 terrorist attacks and, 175–76, 180, 186
Smith, Joseph, 57, 60, 214
  tithing and, 87–88
Smith Barney, 62
Southwest Airlines, 77–78, 158
Speyer, Jerry, 17–18
Staheli, Donald L.:
  management skills of, 45
  Quigley's relationship with, 44, 46–48
  religious beliefs and commitments of, 44–48
Steinbrenner, George, 109
Stevens, Kevin, 104–6
stewardship, 92–93
success:
  competitiveness and, 28–30, 34–35
  finances and, 22–23, 95
  motivations in, 22–23
  preparation in, 35–36
  relationship between obedience and, 9
  wives as secret to, 144–69
Sullivan, Scott, 70
Summers, Larry, 207, 210–12

suppliers:
  and aftermath of 9/11, 196–97
  Rollins's preparation and, 36
  trust and, 72, 78–80
Swartz, Mark, 96
Swiss Air, 195
Swiss Re, 74, 76

Tishman-Speyer, 16–17
tithing, 87–97, 129, 215
  failing to pay, 90–92
  as insulation against greed, 93–97
  stewardship and, 92
tobacco, avoidance of, 59–60, 129, 215
trust, trustworthiness, 70–85
  corporate scandals and, 70–72, 81
  ethical dilemmas and, 73–74
  investors and, 77–78, 80
  and mergers and acquisitions, 75–77
  negotiating and, 79–80
  power and, 106–7
  and Quigley's avoidance of infidelity, 65–66
  taking responsibility in, 82–85
  temptations and, 80–83
Tyco International, 70, 81, 96, 100

Universal Studios, 16–17
Urban Institute, 150
Utah Jazz, 23–24, 126

vacations, 58, 95, 162, 188
Van Gundy, Jeff, 83–84, 107–8
Viacom, 15

Weston Presidio Capital, 77–78
Willes, Mark H., 44
wives:
  adult children of, 58, 162, 166–67, 185–86, 190
  childhoods of, 149, 151, 157
  education of, 9, 146–52, 157, 166–68
  employment of, 147–50, 152
  finances of, 97, 148–50, 152–53, 156–57, 160, 162, 167
  frustrations of, 158–59
  religious beliefs of, xv, 46, 50–51, 55, 128, 146, 150–52, 155, 165–66, 168
  resentment and, 158–59
  as secret to husbands' success, 144–69
  as stay-at-home mothers, 145–62, 167–69
  see also family, family life
Wolff, Rick, ix–xi
Word of Wisdom, 60
WorldCom, 70–71, 81, 100

Young, Brigham, 36, 92, 214